Gay Romance Shifter

Beyond The Paranormal The Werewolf Fantasy Shapeshifter Demon Devil Romance

(Lesbian Transgender Mpreg, And Werewolves Alpha Menage)

Ramón Cornejo

Despite the heartfelt pleas of his wolf, Grant's Alpha remained steadfast, refusing to meet his gaze. The observer experienced a sense of powerlessness as he witnessed Zena tilting her head adorned with a cascade of mahogany curls towards Grant, engaging in the exchange of a confidential jest. She positioned herself on the intricately carved chair adjacent to him, assuming a seated posture while reclining slightly and displaying a confident smile towards the group as they proceeded to arrange themselves in their respective positions.

Grant effectively suppressed the collective clamour generated by the amalgamation of various individual voices by employing a simple gesture of lifting his hand. The individual in question was met with expectant gazes from the assembled individuals, prompting him to cast a warm glance across the room, acknowledging his companions. Upon shifting his gaze towards Daniel, he promptly bypassed him and directed a fleeting glance on Tabitha instead, then resuming his perusal of the assembled multitude. Tabitha sought solace by resting on Daniel's chest, allowing her straight black hair to gently graze the fabric of his t-shirt, a gesture that he appreciated.

Daniel made a conscious effort to avert his gaze from Zena, although he found it challenging due to his instinctual inclination, represented by his wolf, to see physically overpowering her in the parking lot. The individual was able to perceive the presence of her wolf companion, observing it as it casually engaged in the act of licking its paws.

Dear fellow siblings! Grant emitted a loud vocalisation, effectively suppressing the remaining few auditory expressions. We express our gratitude for your presence. Given the collective enthusiasm to commence the pursuit, I shall endeavour to be concise in my communication. Riddick detected the presence of a moose in the western direction, implying that a potential confrontation may result in injury or harm to multiple individuals.

An abrupt, fragmented vocalisation emanated from the assemblage as a sign of endorsement. Daniel remained silent, incapacitated by his injuries to the point that he was unable to inhale or exhale.

Grant initiated the conversation by stating that Rafe, who hails from the northern valley pack, had approached us with a request for solidarity. Rafe acknowledged the pack with a nod of greeting from his position at the table. Automatically, he contracted his well-developed muscles. Daniel displayed a nonverbal gesture of disapproval by rolling his eyes.

Grant further elaborated on the matter, stating, "The dominant individual within their social hierarchy has experienced a demise, however, the contender has not yet regained consciousness, and the injuries sustained seem insurmountable."

A palpable wave of sadness and apprehension permeated the space.

Consequently, the northern pack is significantly lacking in strength. There exist several... Janssen is a prominent individual in the field of study being discussed.

Several individuals expressed their agreement with Grant's assessment of Janssen's leadership ability, as evidenced by their audible inhalations.

However, the establishment of a pack necessitates the presence of an Alpha as well as a multitude of other potential members in order to attain true strength. Merely self-identifying as an alpha and deliberately ensuring the subordination of others does not suffice. It is widely acknowledged that this statement holds veracity.

The pack collectively reiterated, "We possess knowledge of the veracity of this statement."

Therefore, it may be argued that it would be more compassionate to disassemble the treaty that has historically divided our packs and territories, and instead establish a single unified pack.

A collective vocalisation of approval was expressed. From her position at the table, Francine surveyed her surroundings, displaying a pleasant countenance and acknowledging others by affirmative gestures.

Daniel was unable to divert his gaze from Zena. The subject appeared notably tranquil. Her radiance was quite palpable. Several additional individuals appeared to have observed it, including Dirk and Jace, who had consumed the entirety of that bottle of rye.

I am aware that the process of acclimating to a new leadership position typically requires a period of adjustment. I would want to express my sincere gratitude to each and every one of you for creating an environment that has made me feel exceptionally embraced during the past few months. Francine, Riddick, Zena, Dirk, and all individuals addressed, It is important to convey my sincere desire to fulfil all of your needs. The prospect of overseeing a substantial group has long been a personal aspiration, one that holds the potential for significant achievements and fulfilment for all involved parties."

A significant surge of consensus resonated. Francine exhibited a gesture of triumph by raising her clenched hand, accompanied by a facial expression characterized by a broad smile. She extended her arm towards her shoulder and grasped Riddick's hand, gently placing it to her cheek.

Grant, in an attempt to regain control of the situation, raised his arms once more, signaling for silence. He emitted a genial chuckle. Daniel experienced a fluctuation of emotions as he observed his Alpha bestowing affection upon others while neglecting him.

Please pay attention. Grant emitted a loud vocalization, prompting an immediate cessation of noise from everyone present. The individuals' facial expressions became fixed in a smiling position.

In the fifth chapter of the book, the author delves into the subject matter at hand.

Rick engaged in activities with Trevor, who appeared to also be enjoying a day of leisure. The frequency of their interactions had been limited since Rick commenced his employment at the organization. He frequently engaged in nocturnal activities that extended long beyond sunset. During that period, he simply desired to recline in his bed and engage in slumber. He continued to receive infrequent female companions, each distinct from the others, but he consistently rebuffed their advances and dismissed them.

Trevor eventually broached a question that had been avoided by others, as his actions had garnered attention. Rick had assumed the role of Dante's primary confidant, eliciting a sense of envy among individuals who had been associated with Dante for a longer duration. However, Trevor remained the sole individual who maintained a personal connection with Rick. Therefore, it is vital for me to get knowledge about Rick.

Pardon me, could you kindly reiterate your statement?

What is the rationale behind the decision to dismiss the female individuals? Dante hardly bestows such rewards, and when he does, it is expected that one should wholeheartedly accept them. Jazz is highly enticing and difficult to resist.

Rick experienced a sensation of increased warmth in his facial region and expressed a desire for this physiological response to remain imperceptible in terms of any observable alteration in the coloration of his visage. The absence of a comprehensible answer was evident to him. Throughout their extended period of confinement, the two individuals engaged in numerous conversations covering a wide range of topics. However, discussions pertaining to women were noticeably absent from their discourse.

Currently, I am unable to allocate time for that task. The assertion that women alone contribute to creating difficulties is a commonly held belief.

Trevor gazed at the individual, contemplating the veracity of his statements. The individual possessed a sense of doubt, although it was not a matter that was explicitly inquired about, even by himself. I acknowledge your perspective, however, it is advisable to carefully consider the implications before declining a gift.

Certain individuals may perceive it as a form of disrespect or insult.

Rick had not previously considered that perspective; however, he was unable to take any action at that moment. Rick had not sent him a message for several weeks, and he was anticipating that the recipient had perceived the implicit message. He contemplated the possibility of allowing them to remain for a period of time if another one was dispatched in the future. The individual in question did not desire the current circumstances, as he found it undesirable to be subjected to the silent scrutiny of individuals such as Trevor, who were questioning his actions.

I understand your perspective. I failed to consider the matter at hand. I have been experiencing significant fatigue. I shall bear that in mind for future reference. It appears that I seldom experience fatigue.

Trevor displayed a facial expression characterized by the upward curving of the lips, commonly associated with positive emotions. Thus, the aforementioned statement is presented.

The topic was abandoned, albeit not promptly enough to alleviate the discomfort in Rick's thoughts. The situation was becoming increasingly evident that he would need to take action. Not all individuals exhibited the same level of generosity as Trevor, and he was averse to the initiation of something. He needed to locate a romantic partner for himself or a similar alternative. The concerns regarding his romantic relationships were more prevalent among others than within himself.

I am pleased that you have taken me to this location, Trevor. If it were not for your influence, it is likely that I would currently be employed at a McDonald's establishment.

Trevor nonchalantly dismissed him with a wave. You have enhanced my reputation. I was aware of your formidable nature, having witnessed numerous instances of your combat prowess during our time together. However, the current situation surpasses any previous encounters."

Rick simply nodded in agreement. The individual in question was simply fulfilling necessary tasks, yet a certain aspect of his being harbored a desire for Dante's happiness. The individual harbored positive sentiments towards the other person, and the manner in which he had been treated subsequent to his initiation into the group solidified these emotions.

Following a period of leisure and sustenance, Rick returned to the compound where he observed the women engaging in dance on the ground level. There was consistently an abundant quantity of them available for observation. This action undertaken by their intrepid leader served as yet another means to garner support from the group members, and similar to its effect on Rick, it engendered a sense of allegiance. The compound constituted a close-knit community wherein Dante assumed a prominent leadership role, garnering the admiration and reliance of its members. Rick found it challenging to refrain from admiring him due to his exemplary leadership attributes.

Theodore suppressed a lighthearted exclamation as he entered the room hastily upon observing the attractive Omega on the verge of immersing themselves in a considerable amount of chocolate scattered across the floor. Despite the considerable allure of that notion, he was cognizant of the fact that he should refrain from paying attention. The individual expressed a reluctance to experience emotional pain and vulnerability once more.

The individual was aware that it was inappropriate to engage in laughter or entertain the current stream of thoughts, particularly in light of the recent disrespectful behavior exhibited by their purportedly genuine romantic partner, referred to as their Omega, or rather, their former Omega.

Gerry, the individual who has betrayed their allegiance. The individual who was intended to be his life partner ought to have been his eternal companion. The individual to whom he had recently been prepared to express his everlasting affection. Gerry's verbal and behavioral expressions were unequivocally deceptive, serving as mere facades to manipulate the Alpha and achieve his personal objectives. Theo, having gained this awareness, found no solace in this realization, as the entire ordeal remained profoundly humiliating to him.

Theo contemplated the rapidity with which circumstances can alter, adopting a wry perspective. However, he presently observed a positive shift in his situation. The individual experienced a sense of joy within his emotional state, accompanied by an increase in intensity, and subsequently, a more pronounced surge of desire manifested between his robust upper legs.

The individual came to the realization that there would also be a wedding to cancel.

That would constitute a highly embarrassing moment, would it not? However, in the present moment, the individual finds solace and amusement as they observe an endearing Omega, adorned with chocolate, which serves to alleviate their perception of life's difficulties and unpleasantness. The observation appeared to be accurate and quite enjoyable.

Theo was prepared to fully embrace the sensation of sweetness. The protagonist recognized that the likelihood of success was low, yet he did not experience fear or apprehension in the face of potential retribution from the Omega. This response differed from what he would have expected if Gerry had been in a similar comical predicament. Theodore made the determination that the content possessed elements of humor and sensuality. The individual expressed a desire to orally consume the chocolate substance from the small Omega's fragile physique, gradually and systematically, until the Omega was completely devoid of clothing and hygienically prepared. Subsequently, Theo would proceed to establish a possessive relationship with the Omega.

He would engage in the act of procreation, resulting in the formation of a familial unit, by depositing his reproductive fluid into the small orifice, which he would expand using his large reproductive organ. Upon witnessing the aforementioned sight, the individual in question began to experience physiological arousal, as evidenced by the manifestation of an erect state. This response was further intensified by the contemplation of the associated idea.

He anticipated that Alec would not be deterred by his conspicuous physiological response. Nevertheless, despite the potential embarrassment associated with this occurrence, he was unable to allocate mental resources to contemplate such matters due to time constraints. The only action he was able to undertake was relocation.

The situation appeared to be improving, with the potential for further improvement as long as he could prevent the unfortunate occurrence of a spill on his personal kitchen floor, along with the associated untidiness.

Despite his inclination to burst into laughter, he restrained himself due to his unwavering commitment to chivalry. Nonetheless, a stifled chuckle managed to slip through his lips. The slender shopkeeper exhibited a playful demeanor, captivating Theo's attention with his enticing hip movements, evoking a range of provocative thoughts. The individual experienced a physical sensation of increased rigidity, accompanied by a strong and assertive physiological response. This was expressed through a low vocalization in the throat, indicative of a desire to engage in biting, seizing, and mating behaviors. However, the individual exercised self-restraint, choosing to delay these actions for the present moment.

Prior to making any hasty assumptions, it is imperative to clarify that I did not engage in a confrontation with him. What is the rationale behind this request? The reason for my perception is rooted in my emotional intuition, which led me to believe that the level of connection and commitment between Gabriel and myself was insufficient to ensure his loyalty. Observing him engage in an intimate act with someone other than myself elicited a profound sense of emotional distress, depleting any semblance of joy within my heart. Analogous to an empty container, I experienced a profound sense of insignificance. In order to prevent succumbing to the overwhelming disappointment of an unattainable aspiration, I promptly returned to my residence and immersed myself in a state of despair.

I refrained from confiding in Mike regarding my predicament due to my reluctance to involve him in the complications that had arisen as a result of my actions. Moreover, Mike was grappling with his personal inner struggles, and the addition of another one would potentially exacerbate his mental state. Gabriel persistently engaged in telephonic and textual communication with me on subsequent mornings, despite my prior determination to refrain from engaging in dialogue with him. I implemented a measure to prevent further communication by blocking the individual's contact information, and subsequently adopted a strategy of feigning ignorance towards their existence.

Subsequent to our initial interaction, Gabriel ceased all communication with me. The individual in question did not make an effort to visit me, leading me to infer that this lack of action was due to their contentment in their newfound state of liberation. Fortunately, I was able to acquire the support of two additional acquaintances who aided in the alleviation of my emotional distress and anguish: alcohol and sexual activity.

I hold a strong aversion towards all individuals. I vocalized in unison with the resounding music, causing a sensation of auditory discomfort within the confines of our recently established concealed location. The decision was made to depart from the establishment known as Dusk & Dawn and relocate to the Spread Eagle Bar, situated on the opposite side of the city. On a nightly basis, subsequent to my mother's departure for work, I consistently requested that Mike consume a beverage. The individual consistently expressed agreement due to their prevailing sadness, while I, in turn, experienced relief that they refrained from inquiring about my well-being.

Each evening, I am tasked with escorting an intoxicated individual to their place of residence. Successive nights, one following the other. We engaged in an intimate act, disrobed, and shared clandestine moments prior to the arrival of our mother. During the subsequent three-month period, I experienced a profound sense of fulfillment and satisfaction.

I experienced difficulty in ceasing my current activity as I found myself consistently confronted with persistent mental images of Gabriel's visage and cheerful expression whenever I attempted to discontinue said activity. I believed that I had already progressed beyond the emotional state of experiencing distress and shedding tears. However, I have recently come to the realization that I have not yet fully moved on from my attachment to Gabriel, who holds the distinction of being the first individual with whom I engaged in an intimate encounter and remains my sole and irreplaceable romantic interest. Despite my enduring affection for him, it became imperative for me to relinquish my attachment to him. Thus, my indulgence in alcohol persisted.

As the snow began to melt, symbolizing the transition from winter to spring, I made the deliberate choice to invite another individual into my residence. I refrained from inquiring about the gentleman's name as my primary objective was solely to engage in recreational activities. Subsequently, we engaged in an intimate act of kissing, proceeded to disrobe, and entered the confines of my personal quarters. At the moment of our physical union, my mother abruptly entered my bedroom, displaying a countenance filled with displeasure.

Mother! I vocalized with force, exerting physical pressure to create distance between myself and the individual in question, subsequently utilizing a crumpled bed sheet to conceal my unclothed form.

The woman inquired with a sense of astonishment, "Leon, what is the nature of your current actions?" Subsequently, she directed a piercing gaze towards the individual accompanying me. I initially held a skeptical view regarding the veracity of the claims made by others, who asserted that you were regularly hosting a succession of male individuals within this premises on a nightly basis.

Excellent! This is highly commendable. I internally acknowledged. How did I exhibit such a lack of attention to detail? I had intended to fabricate a justification, however, the opportunity for doing so had already elapsed. I rose from a seated position, donned my undergarments, and directed my gaze towards the unclothed individual positioned before me. Mother, this is...

"Dan," he stated with a smile.

"Evacuate from my residence expeditiously, lest I employ my firearm against you," cautioned my mother.

With a sense of fear, Dan awoke and swiftly retrieved his shirt and pants from the floor. Therefore, "Goodbye!" he uttered before abruptly departing from my room.

Inquiring as to the rationale behind your actions, Leon, I am left to ponder the implications of your behavior towards me. After ensuring that Dan had already left the house, Mom inquired. What actions are you engaging in that pertain to your personal well-being?

I nonchalantly raised my shoulders in a gesture of indifference or uncertainty. In a facetious manner, I responded, "Merely engaging in recreational activities."

Do not dare employ such a manner of speech towards me, Leon.

Could you please clarify your statement or question? I am not engaging in any inappropriate behavior, Mother. As an individual who has reached the age of majority, I am now faced with the responsibility of making independent decisions.

My mother elevated her hands in a gesture of capitulation. Leon, it appears that you lack comprehension of my perspective. I am solely ensuring your safety.

Cease uttering such statements, Mother! I vocalized with increased volume. You are failing to provide me with adequate protection.

The mother displayed a facial expression of disapproval. I possessed the knowledge that she lacked the ability to comprehend the perspective from which I was expressing myself. Could you please clarify the subject matter of your discourse?

I initiated the conversation by expressing, 'You provided me with comprehensive details regarding your initial experience of romantic affection, and I placed my trust in your account.' I experienced a heightened sense of imminent emotional volatility. I held a firm conviction in the veracity of all the information conveyed to me, including the idyllic conclusions of fairy tales and the amorous encounters you described. The individual expressed their belief in the promise of receiving an equitable portion of enduring affection, as communicated by the interlocutor.

I was incredulous at the fact that Glenwise was engaging in a romantic embrace with me, yet I was determined to prevent him from discontinuing the act or altering his decision, to the best of my ability.

His lips made contact with mine, eliciting a sensation of warmth and stimulation throughout my skin. Simultaneously, a surge of exhilaration coursed through my veins, causing my blood to circulate rapidly throughout my body. Indeed, a substantial amount of blood had accumulated in my groin area, inadvertently coming into contact with Glenwise's leg.

I assert that I successfully accomplished that task. Indeed, it was Glenwise who had accomplished the task. The individual exerted control over my physical movements akin to that of a puppeteer, firmly grasping me in close proximity, manipulating the positioning of my head as desired, and urging me to partake in oral actions.

I did not require any additional motivation.

The anticipation of this moment had been building within me for numerous years, to the extent that it evoked a sense of familiarity. I had envisioned the scenario in numerous iterations, wherein Glenwise abruptly displayed interest in my presence... On the occasion when Glenwise ultimately expressed his desire for my companionship, and subsequently, the instance when Glenwise claimed possession of me...

The embrace of his arms felt instinctive, prompting a complete absence of cognitive activity, as my sole focus became the desire to further intertwine our bodies. I desired his companionship. This concludes the discussion.

The individual in question did not consider the potential repercussions of their actions, nor did they contemplate their plans for the following day. Furthermore, they neglected to consider minor details such as the proper method for unfastening their trousers.

The idea was conceived by Glenwise.

His hands moved around to my groin and I had a horrific second in which I felt such a burst of pleasure that I wasn't sure whether I'd come or not. Glenwise had his hands on my groin and his tongue finally sliding between my lips to own my mouth, and I had practically died and gone to heaven.

His taste was divine. Heavenly.

My dragon shuddered inside me, wracked with pleasure. I wanted to just give myself to Glenwise on a platter and let him do what he wanted with me, and my dragon was not objecting to that at all. If ever I thought of being with someone else, of kissing them or letting them dominate me, my dragon came roaring up to the surface, filling me, snarling at me that it wasn't going to happen.

With Glenwise, though? My dragon was already his.

His tongue dragged against mine, his taste so delicious that I whimpered and clung to him. He began to growl. The sound vibrated around me, filling me, filling my mouth and making our kiss somehow even more erotic.

I was hearing Glenwise's dragon.

His thrusting tongue became harder, his hands tightened around me, and I was pinned in place and unable to move. Who wanted to move anyway? I was in the best place in the world, and a place I'd never have thought in a thousand years I'd end up.

Within the embrace of Glenwise, I endeavored to deepen my vulnerability, seeking to surrender myself entirely to his possession. To asphyxiate me with his mouth, to forcefully embrace me against his torso. If there were a means by which I could facilitate the insertion of his phallus into my person, it is likely that the resulting euphoria would be so overwhelming as to perhaps lead to my demise.

I did not anticipate his decision to release me. I almost experienced a full loss of balance due to my failure to engage any of my own muscular efforts in maintaining an upright posture. I had been relying heavily on Glenwise. Fortunately, he had recognized this and maintained physical contact with me while I swayed, providing stability and support.

The individual exhibited persistent vocalizations while displaying a fierce countenance, as evidenced by the presence of a dragon-like quality in his gaze, which ignited his eyes with a fervent intensity. The subject's ocular organs exhibited a distinct hue resembling that of pure silver, exhibiting a fluid-like quality akin to molten rock beneath the outer layer.

I was unable to do anything except regard him with a foolish expression. At that very time, I found myself unable to verbalize any words, as my respiratory system was entirely engaged in the act of respiration. at casting his gaze at me, Glenwise exhibited a hostile expression, followed by a sudden descent onto his knees.

In this section, we will delve into the content of Chapter 2.

As the evening approached, Melissa anxiously adjusted her attire, a stunning mermaid-style gown that was tightly laced to enhance her hip contours. Amanda opted for a comparable design using a halter shape that exuded a more casual aesthetic, extending to the floor and trailing behind her. It proved to be challenging to enter the taxi while wearing these garments, particularly due to the sheer nature of the fabric in the intense sunlight in the bustling urban environment.

As the individuals were transported to a higher socioeconomic area, they observed the luminous illumination and opulent establishments exuding affluence and enthusiasm. The individuals in question exhibited a resemblance to rabbits descending into a cavity, akin to two disoriented juvenile lagomorphs being drawn into a realm replete with enchanting gemstones and brittle mineral formations. The exterior of the cab exhibited a remarkable luster, resembling the appearance of neglected leather shoes requiring immediate refurbishment. The costumes exhibited a remarkable level of glamour and conveyed an overt sense of beauty; nonetheless, the individuals wearing them had a profound sense of displacement.

Upon the arrival of the taxi in front of a substantial flight of steps that ascended towards a grand residence, the two women observed the scene intently from within the vehicle until the cab driver requested his fare. A male individual of youthful age approached the entrance and proceeded to perform the action of holding the door ajar, presumably assuming the role of a domestic servant tasked with welcoming the arriving individuals to the social gathering.

In a gentle manner, he directed the ladies up the steps, indicating the way. Upon arrival, you will receive a warm welcome at the entrance.

Experiencing a sense of elation, the two women maintained an elevated posture and ascended the stairs cautiously, exhibiting an air of ownership over a significant portion of global wealth. The activity appeared trivial for adult females, yet their admiration for the landscape compelled them to engage in role-playing.

Upon reaching the uppermost landing, an additional butler proceeded to unlatch the expansive ivory doors adorned with a gilded embellishment. As the doors swung open, an opulent gathering of considerable grandeur unfolded before the observer's eyes. Dahlia, positioned in proximity to the entrance, convened with her dancers in anticipation of their arrival. Several other female individuals had already been consuming champagne and were meandering across the expansive frontal region, which evidently did not exclusively serve as the sole standing location for the gathering.

Women are encouraged to engage in independent exploration. Dahlia proclaimed the presence of a celebration in each area as she lifted her glass.

Amanda and Melissa shared a mutual gaze, contemplating the presence of suitable male individuals with whom they may engage in social activities. The marble flooring exhibited a lustrous sheen beneath a resplendent golden chandelier, with its opulence exceeding its intricacy. The two individuals, identified as women, each acquired a glass of champagne and proceeded to explore the various corridors, expressing their admiration for the opulent velvet carpets that guided them into expansive chambers adorned with gilded vases and roses. The rose stems were adorned with a layer of golden paint. The individuals expressed curiosity over the means by which this gentleman had acquired the resources necessary to host such a delectable gathering, speculating that he may have been born into a privileged background and received education in the ways of opulence. However, it is imperative to ascertain the individual's gender, whether they were male or female. Who was the undisclosed host?

Upon entering the main ballroom, the women, who appeared to be experiencing a sense of being overwhelmed, were met with a diverse array of individuals attired in elegant garments. Simultaneously, a musical ensemble consisting of violinists performed in the background. The entirety of the floor consisted of white and red marble, exhibiting a near-perfect reflection of the ceiling painting. At the opposite side of the room, a buffet was positioned, attracting the women who, although having consumed a meal before to their arrival, experienced a moderate sense of hunger. The individuals partook in the delectable assortment of vegetables and accompanying dips, observing their surroundings as they consumed their food with deliberate and cautious chewing, in order to avoid any potentially embarrassing actions.

Melissa expressed her astonishment at the remarkable beauty of the surroundings while intermittently consuming little portions. It is highly irrational. Have you observed the painting situated prominently featuring an equine figure? Is it plausible to consider whether the individual in question is our host?

I am uncertain about the answer. Amanda expressed her strong desire to change out of her current attire and engage in intimate activities with another individual, while her attention was drawn towards a particularly attractive young man situated in the vicinity.

Hello, Amanda! Please refrain from using offensive language and maintain a respectful tone. In order to participate in the showcase, it is imperative that we exhibit appropriate behavior. Melissa astutely observed that any untamed mischievous activities would undoubtedly lead Dahlia to reassess her position. She placed her plate on the table as the attractive unmarried man approached their vicinity.

The individual positioned himself in front of the group, displaying a charming smile on his face, while his well-groomed hair was meticulously styled to showcase his remarkably balanced facial attributes. The individual possessed a pair of impeccably azure eyes, positioned beneath a set of deeply shaded eyebrows, while their nose exhibited ideal proportions. The gentleman's attire consisted of a luxurious cotton suit, dyed in a deep shade of black reminiscent of the darkness of night. The suit was embellished with a pocket chain made of gold, adding a touch of opulence to the ensemble. Additionally, a golden rose adorned the breast pocket, further enhancing the sartorial elegance.

The individual addressed the women present with refined speech, demonstrating a high level of proficiency in the etiquette and customs of engaging in formal social interactions. May I have the honor of extending a warm welcome to you in the confines of my modest abode. I am Craig Fitzgerald, the proprietor of numerous retail enterprises around the nation and the highest-earning billionaire of the year, as reported by Forbes.

Terry abruptly regained consciousness to find his supervisor's piercing gaze and well-defined physique in close proximity, positioned just beyond the desk.

The individual exhibited a smug expression, suggesting an imminent eruption of laughter in response to a certain stimulus. Could you perhaps clarify the topic or subject you are referring to?

It is possible that Terry is experiencing a dream-like state. The individual blinked, attempting to comprehend the reason behind Mr. F's presence and the peculiar gaze directed towards them. Observing him with heightened curiosity, Terry experienced a sensation of unease and abruptly became aware of his wakefulness, as conveyed by the intensity emanating from the depths of his dark eyes.

The individual assumed an upright position and engaged in stretching exercises, finding it difficult to suppress the physiological reaction resulting from having slept in an uncomfortable posture. To their dismay, they realized that this occurrence took place within the confines of their workplace. The individual is situated at his workstation.

Terry's gaze shifted towards the desk, where he noticed the folder that he had seemingly been using as a makeshift pillow. It became evident, based on the stiffness in his neck, that this had not been a wise decision.

Expletive! He uttered profanities under his breath. The individual has been apprehended. The individual had inadvertently slept off while on duty, specifically at their workstation, situated at their desk, to be precise.

What would Mr.Fennison's perception be at this point? It is likely that he would face termination. Greetings. Following his contemplation of resignation, he subsequently experienced a change of heart, expressing a desire to remain in his current position, aiming to secure a promotion and leave a lasting impression on his superior. However, the current circumstances have presented an unexpected setback.

This approach did not effectively demonstrate competence or professionalism to the supervisor, did it?

Terry expressed satisfaction with his performance, as evidenced by the subtle smirk he experienced inside. However, his attention was soon diverted by an external auditory phenomenon resembling an echo.

Fennison expressed approval, while holding a coffee cup in one hand and the report that Terry dimly recalled completing about two am after discreetly entering Dennison's office to place it on his desk, in the other. Terry recollected the occasion when he had delivered the report and availed himself of the opportunity to occupy his supervisor's seat at the workstation. For a little period of time, he derived a sense of guilty satisfaction from occupying the same seat where his attractive superior typically sat, despite the lack of any meaningful significance. To a certain extent, it had served as a form of compensation for the additional effort exerted by him.

The individual in question refrained from causing any disruptions or engaging in any intrusive behavior. The individual did not have the authority or right to do so. Furthermore, once he successfully apprehended his target, which he was determined to achieve at all costs, he would diligently gather all the necessary information regarding the enigmatic individual who had captivated his emotions. To the extent that the elder gentleman desired to disclose. Terry came to the realization that he was content with the extent to which the man was willing to disclose information.

Terry expressed a strong desire to acquire comprehensive knowledge, including intricate details, about the man in question. However, the pursuit of such information was deemed non-urgent. The individual had believed and desired that they possessed an ample amount of time at their disposal. There was no necessity for him to engage in intrusive or covert activities. The individual has the option to exercise patience. The individual exhibited a sense of patience, or at least believed that he possessed such a trait.

However, all of those aspirations were abruptly shattered when he was discovered napping at his workstation. There is a high likelihood that he would face termination from his employment, would he not?

The individual directed their gaze upwards, seeing the expression of contentment on the countenance of Mr. F, characterized by his ruggedly attractive visage adorned with a slight beard, suggesting a lack of attention to shaving on this particular morning. This might be attributed to the possibility of it being a Saturday or potentially due to the individual's haste in arriving at their current location, the explanation for which remains unspecified. These reports are evidently of significant importance. Alternatively, the matter in question may hold significant importance.

Terry contemplated the insignificance of the situation, although soon thereafter, he experienced a stunning realization as the words uttered by his superior finally permeated his consciousness.

Excellent work!

Terry displayed a negative response by shaking his head.

Expressing gratitude, the individual eventually managed to utter, "Thank you, sir," while simultaneously shaking their head in disagreement.

Did you have a challenging evening? Fennison inquired, accompanied by a suggestive expression, seemingly cognizant of his capacity to have subjected Terry to a more intense evening.

Terry experienced a physiological response characterized by a reddening of the face when contemplating the aforementioned idea, while simultaneously perceiving a facial expression from his superior characterized by the upward curving of the lips.

In the eighth chapter of the book, the author delves into the subject matter at hand.

The sun ascended to a considerable altitude in the atmosphere before to their awakening. The individuals had succumbed to slumber while occupying the same couch. He extended his arm to encircle her shoulders, causing her to recline in close proximity to his lap. Both individuals were taken aback by the sudden and forceful knocking on the door. The woman's immediate reaction was to swiftly move towards the opposite end of the home, but the man intervened and prevented her from doing so.

He softly whispered, "Proceed to the basement with a quiet gait," prior to releasing her.

The individual cautiously proceeded towards the basement, adopting a tiptoeing gait. However, upon reaching the entrance, they paused in order to engage in auditory surveillance.

May I inquire further? at opening the door, the individual had a sense of relief at sighting the food bags.

I have received the list you provided.

I had anticipated your presence throughout the previous evening.

I became overly engrossed or excessively enthusiastic. I apologize for my actions.

Thank you. The individual proceeded to acquire the luggage and subsequently retreated, with the other person closely trailing and thereafter closing the door.

Have you engaged in any romantic or sexual relationships with any of the girls?

The absence of sound or noise.

Do you intend to make a genuine attempt to purchase any of them?

The absence of sound.

Sir, may I inquire as to the reason for your consistent reticence? The statement is perceived as vexing.

The sole task assigned to you was the delivery of this item, without any obligation to remain thereafter.

I would like to inquire about the status of our intrepid leader.

Following his departure, Mary ascended from the basement and cautiously surveyed her surroundings from the adjacent corner.

"What?" he stared at her with an intense expression.

The absence of any discernible content or substance is evident in the statement provided.

He raised an eyebrow.

I concur. The perceived tone of the statement appeared to be condescending.

This observation should not be unexpected. He expresses a desire to obtain the position I currently hold. I am unable to comprehend the rationale behind his actions, yet he does.

Perhaps he enjoys the company of women?

He emitted a light-hearted laugh, expressing his belief that the individual in question desires to explore new avenues or areas of interest. Given that this cargo only consists of females, it is important to acknowledge that not all individuals possess a preference for women.

Mary gazed intently for a little duration, but subsequently acknowledged the concept when she comprehended it. She retrieved one of the bags and proceeded downstairs, simultaneously dragging a garbage can alongside her. The individual in question exhibited a conscientious attitude towards waste management, ensuring that the presence of refuse did not exacerbate the existing hardships experienced by the underprivileged young women. Upon her ascent to the upper level, she discovered that he was engaged in the act of culinary preparation. She positioned herself next to him and starting assisting.

You possess a rigid demeanor. May I inquire about the source of your culinary expertise?

Observing the actions of others.

"It appears that you were engaged in the observation of robotic entities," she offered a kind smile and playfully poked him, although he maintained a composed demeanor and persisted with his tasks. Are there any additional items that you engage in smuggling?

Could you please clarify or provide further explanation?

The game in question was left incomplete.

Are you now engaged in ongoing efforts to evade capture or confinement?

The response provided by the user is negative in nature.

Satisfactory. None of you are.

The individual displayed a nonverbal gesture of disapproval by rolling her eyes and emitting an audible exhalation of frustration. An apparent source of agitation was affecting him, albeit she lacked knowledge of its nature. The individual expressed a desire to ascertain the matter in order to rectify it. The sensation elicited amazement within her. What are the potential factors contributing to my current condition? As she engaged in the process of painstakingly scrambling eggs and disregarded the audible sizzling emanating from the bacon, she posed a question to herself. The individual had exhibited a slightly more magnanimous approach towards his provision of meals subsequent to granting her considerable freedom to move about the premises. However, it remained the case that she was unable to venture outside the confines of the residence.

Mary saw the scene outside through the window, displaying a facial expression of displeasure. It can be inferred that the individual accompanying her noticed her reaction, as they gently nudged her and raised an eyebrow, silently seeking clarification. The subject displayed a gentle grin and refrained from engaging in a series of inquiries, which was unlike of her usual behavior. The eggs were placed on the enormous platter, and subsequently, the individual patiently awaited the arrival of the bacon. In addition, he had another matter in progress, albeit in a secondary position, nevertheless she refrained from interrogating him. She desired to introduce a subtle alteration in order to maybe facilitate her endeavor to evade. The individual was beginning to contemplate their desire to terminate the relationship.

He inquired with curiosity, "Are you being quiet?"

Yes. She displayed a facial expression of happiness towards him and proceeded to take hold of the plate. Mary promptly descended the stairs and distributed the food with meticulous attention to ensure equitable distribution among all individuals present. Subsequently, she ascended to the upper level of the premises in order to engage in the task of dishwashing. The individual expressed contentment in having an activity to engage in, as opposed to idling away in the basement.

Shortly thereafter, she discovered him seated on the couch, engrossed in his tablet once more, his countenance displaying a disconcerted expression. She positioned herself next to him and attempted to gaze over the tablet, although the contents displayed on the device were incomprehensible to her. The individual averted her gaze and emitted a gentle exhalation.

"What?" he murmured as she rested her head against his shoulder.

I am experiencing a sense of unfamiliarity and peculiarity in my surroundings, giving rise to a feeling of unease and uncertainty. I am unable to ascertain any information on your identity or background.

A considerable passage of time transpired, estimated to be perhaps two or three months. Determining the precise duration of the day and nocturnal periods on Bellafoss proved to be an insurmountable challenge, with a noticeable lack of assistance from others who displayed a disinterest in aiding her in this endeavor. Rachel had recently begun to permit time to become indistinct. Although she did not receive daily invitations to Rold's aerial intimate space, she held a distinct position as his most preferred companion.

The remaining ladies developed a strong aversion for her as a result of her behavior, although they refrained from attempting to assert dominance over her once more. The initial spouse appeared to acknowledge that Rachel has superior physical attributes and displayed a lack of enthusiasm towards experiencing another instance of facial injury.

Brook informed Rachel that Myra had her face bandaged for an extended duration prior to being discharged from the hospital. The protagonist's social circle consisted solely of one individual who engaged in conversation with her, namely her sole friend, and Tuo, who, despite being restricted from engaging in substantial interactions with the wives, also played a role in their social dynamic. The remaining spouses clandestinely exchanged derogatory remarks behind her, or alternatively, they exhibited apprehension and deliberately steered clear of her presence. No other individuals were encountered by them, even following an extended duration. However, other individuals resided within the dwelling, situated at a lower elevation in proximity to the mountainous terrain. The individuals in question were of lower social status and were strictly prohibited from accessing the upper chambers occupied by the sister wives and their husband, Rold.

"Agreed," responded Rachel after engaging in a period of contemplation. The individual derived satisfaction from the knowledge that the initial spouse, identified as Myra, was confined to a foreign medical facility. I possess an additional response for individuals who engage in confrontational behavior towards me, which is even more severe.

Indeed, it is evident that you have been maintaining your physical fitness. Do you engage in frequent physical activity when you are in solitude?

If it is necessary for you to be informed, I do engage in the practice of kickboxing. However, I obtain a sufficient amount of physical activity via engaging in solitary activities with my spouse.

Brook displayed a smile in response, exhibiting a slight blush. She exhibited a lesser inclination to engage in discussions pertaining to sexual matters compared to several other wives who were more forthcoming. Rachel appreciated this aspect of herself, as she would have felt very self-conscious discussing her instinctual and intense response to Rold's physically fit physique and well-endowed genitalia. According to Brook, Liliana has informed him that Rold has departed earlier today.

The individual in question exhibits apprehension towards my presence. Could you please clarify your statement? The individual did not communicate any information regarding the matter to me.

Observe her behavior, as she presents herself as if Rold is just her spouse. A neighboring speaker expressed, "You are merely the most recent fad, derogatory term." The individuals were positioned on a chair situated at a considerable distance from the window, and the surrounding space lacked adequate illumination. One of the spouses, specifically the individual with a larger physique and prominent mammary glands, who had made an attempt to forcefully assume the position of being the second person to engage in oral-genital contact with Rachel, was surreptitiously listening to a conversation. It appears that she had stealthily approached the wall.

Rachel exclaimed, "What is the nature of your current actions?"

Brook delicately inquired, "Josie, may I inquire about the whereabouts of your manners?"

Josie expressed her skepticism over the genuine fondness you claim to have for your replacement with great intensity. She likely provided considerable enjoyment for Rold, given her physical attributes and ample comfort for him to engage with. She exhibited a notable tendency towards being unpleasant, and Rachel inferred that she was perceived as a mere object of sexual gratification in the eyes of their shared spouse. However, her frequency of being welcomed to his room was much lower compared to Rachel and Brook.

Why don't you consider socializing with one of Myra's acquaintances, Josie? Rachel rose to her feet and adopted a condescending gaze towards the individual in question. It appears that you are currently experiencing a lack of sexual intimacy with Rold.

An additional altercation occurred later that evening, prior to the ladies' withdrawal to their own chambers.

Josie exhibited initial hesitation, yet ultimately disengaged from Rachel's presence. Subsequently, a diminutive mirror affixed to the wall, characterized by its excessively embellished design, was propelled towards Rachel's cranium. The object narrowly avoided causing significant harm to her, and it broke into pieces upon impact with the wall adjacent to her location, where she remained seated and engaged in conversation with Brook.

Rachel swiftly rotated her head in a state of astonishment, endeavoring to identify the individual responsible for the act of throwing, while the frame, which remained undamaged, emitted a resonant clanging sound upon impact with the floor. I vehemently expressed my intention to cause harm to Josie upon realizing her presence. The assailant successfully delivered a forceful blow to the vulnerable woman's forehead, subsequently incapacitating her by striking her crotch with a knee, causing her to fall to the ground. The adversary exhibited minimal resistance, suggesting a lack of strategic foresight in anticipating this potential outcome.

Tuo employed a method of inducing intense discomfort through the activation of their collars. He applied the same treatment to all of the spouses, including those who were in a state of relaxation or slumber, within the communal space.

After being guided by Tuo, Rachel reclined upon her bed. He had prioritized taking Josie to bed initially, ensuring her well-being. The female individual had a high level of resilience, as she did not sustain any injuries while being subjected to a physical impact.

She vociferously expressed her inability to endure the situation any longer to him. He positioned himself adjacent to the shut entrance, anticipating her entry into the bathing facility. I am not engaging in the act of cleansing my body for your benefit this evening, you contemptible individual.

Rachel, I understand that you are experiencing distress, nevertheless, I am unable to depart until you are adequately prepared for our superior. The fact that he is currently engaged in business-related activities is inconsequential.

The primary source of distress for her was the realization that she would unequivocally be unable to reunite with her spouse. Furthermore, she was deeply dismayed by the fact that she had genuinely regarded him as her legitimate spouse. I desire a restoration of the previous state of affairs. The individual expresses a lack of comprehension of the experience of being forcibly removed from one's residence and compelled to endure a convoluted and perplexing ordeal.

"Yes, I do, without a doubt," said Tuo in a straightforward manner. The individual positioned himself on the floor adjacent to the entrance, displaying a reluctance to fully embrace a state of relaxation. However, this marked the greatest extent to which he had allowed himself to lower his defenses in her presence.

Apologies... You often exhibit a high degree of willingness to accommodate others, often causing me to overlook the fact that you possess some characteristics that are commonly understood."

There were approximately twenty-seven individuals present in the dining room. Alternatively, should he consider not only inanimate objects included into the aesthetic arrangement or depicted in artworks, but also real individuals and their possessions?

Xanran inclined his head upwards and casually directed his gaze towards the ceiling.

Greetings, it has come to my attention that there existed an additional entity, discreetly positioned within the central region of the embellishments situated above his cranium.

Rogan, in a brusque manner, encouraged him to increase his food consumption by placing an additional tiny meat pie onto his plate.

Xanran's fatigue rendered him incapable of engaging in any activity other than fixating his gaze upon the proffered sustenance.

The individual possessed a vague recollection of his acquaintances assisting him in returning to his place of residence, as well as his subsequent deep slumber upon succumbing to unconsciousness. The issue at hand pertained to the individual's lack of rejuvenation. He experienced a severe headache, akin to the rhythmic beating of a drum. The individual exhibited signs of restlessness, with the pained expression on Rodner's face lingering in his mind. Despite consuming the remaining portion of the curative elixir, the desired therapeutic effects were not achieved. He was really exhausted.

However, concurrently, he was unable to remain idle and refrain from taking action.

The individual expressed the need to engage in conversation with the aforementioned person, resulting in a sudden cessation of the subdued conversations taking place in the surrounding vicinity.

Rogan expressed reservations with the proposed idea.

I concur. Fortuitously, we encountered him within a communal setting. Saainren's guard concurred, stating that in the event of another encounter, there is a possibility of his causing harm to you.

Mexi expressed his anger by stating, "You imply causing harm to him once more," while displaying signs of anxiety through the action of tugging at his braid.

Xanran exerted a considerable amount of effort to lower his head and directed his gaze towards his three colleagues. The individual made direct eye contact for the first time since awakening in the late morning.

The individual expressed the need to engage in a conversation with him, reiterating their statement at a deliberate pace.

The significance of this matter cannot be understated. The individual was compelled to undertake the action. The individual in question was unable to depart in a casual manner, as Saainren responded with a resolute tone, expressing a negative response.

Is it not the case? However, it was necessary for him to have this. He was consistently provided with the necessary resources. He directed his gaze towards Rogan, nevertheless, his facial expression remained impassive. Undoubtedly, he provided his unwavering support to his prince. Mexi's countenance contorted with animosity directed towards a someone whom he solely perceived as a foe. Xanran was acquainted with a someone from his past who shown qualities of dedication, diligence, and commitment, rather than being seen solely as a buddy or romantic partner.

Negative.

The response provided unequivocally indicated a negative answer.

A slight smile appeared on his face inadvertently. The disguise that he believed he had abandoned.

The individual acknowledged the validity of the opinions expressed by others, expressing a sense of resignation and disappointment. Subsequently, they gently stood up from the table. I am experiencing a state of physical and emotional discomfort. I shall return to our shared accommodation.

The individuals involved in romantic relationships exchanged fleeting glances, prompting Mexi to assertively express their thoughts.

I also intend to participate. Weix presented me with a book containing a collection of fairytales, and I am eagerly anticipating the opportunity to peruse its contents.

Indeed. He was under surveillance.

I kindly request that you engage in the act of reading aloud for my benefit.

Xanran effectively conveyed a sense of eagerness that was not genuinely felt.

He passively occupied himself for the remainder of the day, engaging in minimal activity. A crowd of individuals surrounded him, exacerbating his already heightened state of anxiety. Upon the arrival of nightfall, when the individuals proceeded to retire to their sleeping quarters, Xanran conscientiously positioned himself at the periphery of the assemblage of individuals. Ultimately, his dorsal region remained in the process of recuperation, and they all engaged in affectionate physical contact with great intensity.

The departure of his friends into the realm of dreams facilitated his ability to surreptitiously depart many hours later.

Without delay, he proceeded with assurance through the various chambers until he reached the foyer, which housed the gateway leading to the external realm.

Upon his arrival to the intricately designed door, he experienced the sensation of a somebody moving in his vicinity, causing him to tense up and become ensnared in the moment.

"What an opportune moment to embark on a leisurely walk," Vitorous remarked languidly.

The individual expressed that the matter in question was not within the purview of the interlocutor, while being cognizant of the potential consequences of the wizard disclosing the information, which would impede his ability to distance himself from the situation.

Indeed, is it not?

The elf, who was causing great frustration, remained in place without raising any alarm, potentially indicating a possibility for rational discourse.

What is your desired outcome or objective? Xanran inquired abruptly.

The companionship of your acquaintances may at times be excessively domineering, but I believe their suggestion of abstaining from alone ventures holds validity.

What is the main argument or thesis you are trying to convey?

Vitorous suggested that it would be advisable to have Weix along.

The auditory perception resembled that of a someone loaning a watchdog. Alternatively, a toy could be considered. Xanran clenched his teeth, yet the notion possessed genuine value. The individual in question did not exhibit a lack of intelligence. Rather, they possessed a cognizance of the potential negative outcomes that could arise from the scenario at hand. Consequently, they expressed a willingness to accompany a someone who would provide support and guidance, while maintaining a sufficient level of detachment to prevent any significant errors in judgment.

Vitorous displayed a smile in response to him.

I intend to rouse him from slumber. He leisurely walked towards the entrance that led to the remaining portion of the Dungeon, casually tossing a remark as he did so. If you are not present upon my arrival, I shall rouse your jovial group of companions.

Xanran remained stationary.

Weix joined the individual a few minutes subsequent to the aforementioned occurrence, while still in the process of removing the residual effects of sleep from his ocular organs.

Xanran initiated the conversation with a greeting, but faced uncertainty in proceeding further due to the lack of knowledge of the extent of information conveyed to the other dragon.

Greetings. Weix displayed a smile towards him. I am pleased that Vitorous roused me from slumber. I may have engaged in an extended discourse with him over the extent of my concerns for your well-being.

Xanran experienced a fleeting sense of remorse as he contemplated the potential distress his absence would cause his romantic partners.

In this section, we will go into the content of Chapter Four.

Kindly disregard Hubert. The individual in question has been employed by the company for a considerable duration, during which he occasionally displays lapses in etiquette. As they entered his office, Romulus provided an explanation. Upon entering the premises, he released his grip on Felix and extended a friendly facial expression towards him. I am pleased that you were able to attend... I found your résumé to be really intriguing. The individual's facial expression transitioned from a genuine smile to a cunning smirk while uttering this statement. Kindly take a seat. The individual's spoken tone exhibited a sense of determination as he issued an authoritative directive, gesturing towards a selection of opulent seating arrangements arranged in close proximity to his desk.

Without delay, Felix complied with his command, exhibiting signs of self-restraint by biting the corner of his lip in an attempt to maintain composure. The individual experienced a sensation of intense heat across his entire body. The individual was unable to articulate the sensation that was within him. Upon the initial contact initiated by Romulus, a sensation akin to the flow of electric current permeated his entire being, resulting in a pronounced physical weakness in his lower extremities. The individual ingested audibly and made an effort to maintain his spatial orientation. What were the factors contributing to the sensation of weightlessness experienced by the individual in response to the presence of this aesthetically pleasing male?

May I inquire about the circumstances behind the state of your shirt? Romulus inquired with courtesy, his keen gaze discerning the blemish on Felix's chest. Immediately, a flush of humiliation caused his cheeks to become a shade of crimson.

The individual hesitated before speaking, exhibiting a momentary pause in their verbal expression. He attempted to articulate his thoughts, but ultimately struggled to do so, resulting in incoherent speech. He berated himself internally while gazing up at the attractive individual, who was currently assuming a relaxed posture against his desk. The individual had rolled up the sleeves of his dress shirt, revealing a tattoo sleeve extending from his shoulders to his elbows. Felix, displaying signs of anxiety, attentively traced the intricate contours of the depicted visuals while his hands involuntarily clenched into fists, resting upon his lap.

Romulus traversed the room with forceful steps, effectively narrowing the distance between the individuals. The individual proceeded to take a seat on the chair positioned nearby, thereafter drawing it nearer to Felix. He delicately positioned his hand on Felix's shoulder, applying a gentle pressure. Please endeavor to compose yourself and regain a state of tranquility. Felix emitted a subdued gasp at perceiving the subtle sensation of electric sparks permeating his dermal layer once more. I do not inflict severe harm through biting. Romulus bestowed a subtle gesture of acknowledgement to the younger individual prior to rising from his seated position. If the individual desires... I consistently carry additional clothing in my possession. I am able to provide you with a loan of one item. Perhaps it will alleviate your anxiety. Romulus proffered his assistance as he proceeded towards a storage space.

Felix attentively observed the subject's actions while experiencing an increased heart rate. The individual has not previously experienced such emotions. Felix believed that he was failing to create a favorable impression. Romulus proceeded to access the entrance and retrieved a blouse of a lavender hue. He displayed a smile before approaching his prospective employee and extended his hand towards him. Please attempt to put it on... it is expected to be suitable for your size... The garment is quite constricting on my body nonetheless.

Felix cautiously accepted the garment and proceeded to survey his surroundings. Could you kindly inform me of the whereabouts of a restroom facility? He inquired, with a sudden surge of self-consciousness.

Romulus emitted a subdued chuckle. Please refrain from withholding information regarding your level of shyness. Romulus exhibited a forward inclination, deftly unfastening the buttons of his suit jacket and facilitating its removal off the individual's shoulders. I am willing to avert my gaze if you like... nonetheless, it is important to acknowledge that we are both male individuals in this context. Romulus proceeded to deliver a second wink at Felix.

Felix experienced an accelerated heart rate and increased perspiration due to his heightened state of anxiousness. The perceived lack of propriety during the interview was juxtaposed with a simultaneous feeling of exhilaration, as the prospect of being bare-chested in the presence of an affluent and attractive individual proved to be invigorating. Without additional contemplation or self-doubt, Felix initiated the deliberate process of unfastening the buttons on his shirt.

Romulus observed the scene with a countenance that conveyed a sense of satisfaction. Upon the removal of the man's shirt, a subtle expression of satisfaction manifested on his countenance. The individual held great admiration for Felix's well-defined and sculpted physical form. Despite being smaller in stature compared to Romulus, the man exhibited a commendable level of physical fitness. Romulus experienced a sense of satisfaction as he contemplated the physical sensations that would be elicited from the man in the hypothetical scenario of being restrained beneath his own body or positioned in a bent-over stance against a desk. A surge of exhilaration coursed through his physique in response to his provocative musings. Consequently, he rose from his seat and discreetly relocated himself to a position behind the desk, seeking to conceal the burgeoning arousal.

Meanwhile, Felix exerted considerable effort to concentrate on the current assignment. Upon successfully removing his own clothing, he had unexpected difficulty in donning the garment bestowed upon him by the Chief Executive Officer. Here. Allow me to provide assistance. The operation of the buttons may present challenges. Romulus expeditiously approached Felix. He positioned himself in close proximity, such that Felix was able to detect the fragrance of his aftershave. The individual experienced a physical reaction, characterized by shuddering and breath-holding, in response to Romulus' action of lowering his head and proceeding to fasten the buttons on the shirt in a deliberate manner.

Larissa's focus was suddenly diverted from her reclined position on the floor, as she lifted her eyes with a sense of astonishment. Before this, her nasal region had been in immediate proximity to the translucent surface made of filmglass. She abstained from rapidly ascending, similar to a disobedient child caught in the process of stealing sweets. It is imperative that you maintain self-control, Larissa. The ability for humans to perceive or comprehend the ideas or intents that reside within one's mind is inherently limited. The persons in question seem to lack awareness regarding your aim to conduct a study of the club premises with the purpose of identifying appropriate male companions. Despite your lack of complete self-awareness on the nature of your acts.

The exclamation conveys a robust emotional response characterized by feelings of displeasure or disappointment. I was unable to detect your presence. Greetings, Floyd. May I ascertain whether you are the intended recipient of this correspondence? She asked, "What is the rationale behind your presence in this particular location?" Entry to the topcourt ballroom is limited exclusively to individuals who are not employed by the organization. The current state of the subject suggests that it is presently undergoing a process of renovation.

In a somewhat negligent manner, she removed her breasts from the floor's surface, where they had been subjected to pressure. She proceeded to readjust her elegant necklace, ensuring that it was positioned symmetrically on her chest, before rising to a standing position.

The resilient person, dressed in a metallic uniform, issued a contemptuous sound through his nostrils, resulting in the formation of wrinkles on his weathered face as his gaze became focused on the exposed portion of her clothing, where her bosom extended beyond the conservative neckline. The current financial condition of Airskayt is characterized by insolvency. I incurred a knee injury upon impact during landing. I proceeded to notify the management. The stranger purported to have perceived your existence and remarked upon the activation of your tracking gadget. May I question about the purpose of your presence in this particular location?

The individual in question demonstrated a lack of concern or attention towards that specific issue. It is praiseworthy that they voluntarily divulged my whereabouts to everyone who requested it. I intend to initiate a conversation with the security personnel.I am not an ordinary individual; instead, I hold the highest level of seniority among the employees inside your organization. And your friend as well, is that accurate? Whom else do you have available for conversation in this vicinity?

The entirety of the galaxy. The individual gestured with her arms. Take a moment to observe your surroundings, Floyd. I am employed at the preeminent establishment within the nightclub industry on Jax-9. I possess the ability to engage in conversations with individuals of my choosing at any given moment. If one desires to repel a multitude of peculiar sexual propositions from many unfamiliar individuals. I do not possess such inclination. Alternatively, I desire to obtain further information regarding the aforementioned extraterrestrial beings. There is no existing company. I am fatigued by the frequent presence of these individuals. The individuals in question exhibit discourteous and deceitful behavior, characterized by their unkind and untrustworthy nature.

That is sufficient, Floyd. She attempted to disregard the persistent nature of his attention, which appeared to be focused on her chest, specifically the slight elevation of her neckline just above the aureolas of her nipples. The individual in question exhibits characteristics commonly associated with an elderly person who lacks cleanliness and hygiene. She experienced a slight sense of sympathy towards him. May I inquire about your current state of well-being? Has everything been proceeding without any issues here? There appears to be a relatively low incidence of altercations occurring within the gambling establishments. Is your health in satisfactory condition?

It can be inferred. The individual exhibited a refusal to allow the subject to remain altered. Please refrain from asserting that you are indifferent, Lady Larissa. You and I share a similar background. Both of us belong to families of pure blood, with ancestral ties dating back to the first colonists. The individuals belonging to your community possess aesthetically pleasing and affluent qualities, whereas those inside my community do not possess such attributes. However, this distinction is inconsequential. The significance of blood is of utmost importance. Does it ever have an impact on you? There has been a significant decline in human presence in this area following the collapse of the gates.

No, it is inconsequential. I appreciate the inclusive environment provided by my club, which serves as a sanctuary on Jax-9, offering individuals from around the galaxy a refuge from potential harassment. The individuals in question endured significant persecution prior to the implementation of the change, Floyd. The situation is really unfavorable.

He continued with determination. I have not observed you in the company of others. The individual is experiencing feelings of ennui and social isolation. How much time has elapsed since you last engaged in a social outing with an aesthetically appealing and sophisticated gentleman? Observe your current state, displaying a confident and assertive demeanor. He gestured towards her chest, causing Larissa to gasp and exhibit a visible blush in response to his boldness. At the age of thirty-six, she was not aware that she still possessed the ability to experience blushing.

Floyd proceeded with a scowl on his face. If you were not significantly younger than me, I would personally pursue a romantic relationship with you. And with whom are you going to choose—one of them? It is advisable to use caution and avoid frequenting this location in most instances. The individual returns to their place of residence. It is advisable to avoid frequenting this establishment. It is evident that your affluent family has financed the acquisition of this property, presumably driven by a specific motivation that eludes my comprehension. However, it is not an appropriate environment for a young girl with good upbringing. There are questionable activities taking place in this situation. It is advisable to seek a suitable male companion. Seek out locations that are deemed secure. Utilize an online matchmaking platform. This is the manner in which I discovered Julloo, whose spirit I hope will never cease to exist.

The individual in question proceeded to fold her arms across her thoracic region, adopted a stern gaze directed towards the subject, briefly contemplated the immediate termination of his employment, and thereafter erupted into a fit of laughter. Floyd, at times, you exhibit behavior that is perceived as bothersome due to your advanced age. I am uncertain as to the rationale to retaining your presence. Indeed, I must acknowledge that you possess the ability to skillfully execute the Freezing Split technique. Please refrain from further discussion regarding my lack of romantic involvement. Let us arrange for a medical professional specializing in orthopedics to examine your knee.

In the seventh chapter

Leon hobbled over to position himself in front of Suzette. It is necessary for you to extend an apology to him.

The individual expressed contemptuous disbelief. May I request an apology? What sort of misguided notion do you currently possess in your mind?

The individual in question is my romantic partner, and it is expected that you offer an apology to him. Leon approached her with purpose, positioning himself in such close proximity that their bodies were on the verge of making contact. He gazed intently into her eyes. Moreover, I do not possess a lack of intelligence.

Is that so? She swiftly moved away. The individual's hair exhibited a vibrant hue of orange, resembling a flowing wave that evoked the imagery of a sweeping flame. She positioned herself adjacent to my location, and her hand swiftly grasped the upper edge of the headboard. Placing three thousand individuals at risk of execution is an action that might be deemed unwise or lacking in sound judgment. Regarding what topic or subject matter are you referring to? Is there a male child present? What is the duration of your acquaintance with him? Due to the absence of any information or communication on him, I am not familiar with his current status or whereabouts.

He faced an equivalent level of peril from Lionshead as I did. I would want to highlight that their state of being lost was already established before to our arrival at this location.

Proximity sufficient for engaging in firearm discharge. The proximity was sufficient to allow visual perception.

Leon had a physical response by tightly gripping and releasing his fists while simultaneously shaking his head. Could you kindly provide me with a reminder, Aunt Suz, of the specific duties and responsibilities expected of me in my role as a guard, as it seems that I am currently experiencing difficulty comprehending them.

No, it appears that you are not. Fortunately, she abandoned the headboard and proceeded towards Max. The individual displayed a reflexive response upon experiencing a sudden tactile stimulation when the woman forcefully placed her hand on his shoulder. Greetings, my name is Max.

The individual in question is named Paolo. The individual in question. The individual in question. Leon, it is your responsibility to ensure the protection of every individual within our collective. The individual proceeded to shut her eyes. The actions you have taken have had a detrimental impact on the collective well-being, perhaps undermining the sacrifices made by your parents.

Could you please cease your current actions? Leon awkwardly moved closer and gently removed her hand off Max's shoulder. I possess comprehensive knowledge on the actions undertaken by my parents for the betterment of our family. For the entirety of the collective. There is no necessity for you to consistently reiterate this point whenever I engage in actions that are not aligned with your preferences.

Can you confirm your level of knowledge on this matter? Based on my observation, it does not appear to be the case. You exhibit a propensity toward imprudent behavior.

Similar to the mother?

She clenched her hands and then unclenched them, mirroring Leon's actions. Please refrain from providing information regarding my sister. I possessed a more comprehensive understanding of her than you could ever attain.

Do you possess knowledge or awareness of the subject matter being discussed? Subsequently, one would recollect the audacious nature exhibited by her as she ventured to the forefront beside her father. He displayed a negative response by moving his head in a deliberate and measured manner. I distinctly recall the statement she made to me, and I am confident that you too have this memory. You were situated in close proximity, for the sake of argument.

Indeed, I possess knowledge of the statement made by the individual in question. With a forceful gesture, she forcefully extended her skeletal finger towards the precise midpoint of Leon's thoracic region. Please refrain from involving them in this matter. The statement posits a stark contrast between the two subjects under consideration.

By what authority do you presume to assert such a claim? It is unlikely that you possess the necessary comprehension to grasp the subject matter. You have not had any prior experiences with individuals.

She administered another forceful slap to his cheek. The audacity of your actions is quite astounding. I am entitled to a higher level of respect than what has been shown to me.

I have the same sentiment.

Cease. Experiencing a sensation of discomfort, a sharp sensation of agony traversed my thoracic region, compelling me to rise upright. Max sent a brief, disapproving look in my direction, his facial expression marked by furrowed brows and prominent creases around his mouth. However, he refrained from taking any action to impede my progress. One advantageous aspect. I positioned myself in close proximity to Leon and made direct eye contact with his aunt. One is entitled to express their thoughts or opinions towards me. Please express any opinions or thoughts you may have regarding my person.

Leon placed his hand gently across my shoulder. Please, Tony. Please allow me to manage the situation involving her.

The individual in question is displaying a lack of attentiveness towards your communication, hence it is possible that they may exhibit a greater receptiveness towards my own discourse.

The individual emitted a snorting sound. What is the rationale behind engaging in such an action? What is your knowledge on the characteristics and attributes of our community?

I expressed my disagreement by shaking my head. There is no significant information or content available. However, I can provide you with the following information: I witnessed Silver committing a homicide. I refrained from continuing my actions. During my observation, I witnessed Leon engage in an act of homicide while assuming the form of a mythical creature known as a unicorn. However, I maintain a sufficient level of concern for him to advocate on his behalf. Until he had the opportunity to provide an explanation, at the very least. Subsequently,I had an optimistic expectation regarding my appreciation of his explanation.

I descended rapidly through the atmospheric layers, precisely at the moment when I visually detected my enduring companion on the verge of being subjected to an attack by a D'naro dragon's stinger in the rear vicinity. The D'naro tribe of dragons exhibited a dark pigmentation, rendering them visually inconspicuous during nocturnal combat scenarios. Moreover, their tails terminated in stingers capable of delivering a potent venom, potent enough to lethally affect dragons of considerable age and prowess, such as Lorsan.

In a spontaneous manner, I impulsively initiated an action by verbally expressing myself, resulting in the discharge of an electrical discharge in the form of a lightning bolt. The D'naro was struck precisely at the moment when its stinger was descending, potentially penetrating Lorsan's resilient dorsal region. The D'naro entity confiscated my electrical discharge and experienced a lateral displacement to the right, while its appendage designed for delivering venomous attacks exhibited erratic movements but failed to make contact with any target. The entity emitted a shrill vocalization characterized by a combination of exasperation and distress.

The auditory perception of a screeching sound consistently elicited a positive emotional response, resulting in the manifestation of a smile on my face. The conflict with the D'naro had persisted for an extensive duration, spanning beyond my recollection. Furthermore, their intellectual capacity appeared to remain stagnant. While it is true that they exhibit increased aggression, their level of intelligence does not demonstrate a significant improvement.

Lorsan, are you in a satisfactory condition?

I am in a satisfactory state. Thank you for providing support.

Certainly, sibling.

Upon conducting a visual survey of the atmosphere, I failed to detect any additional aerial presence of the D'naro individuals, who are derogatorily referred to as "scum." I positioned myself onto the summit of a precipice, affording a panoramic view of the vast expanse of the ocean, with the lifeless remains of a D'naro individual lying in close proximity to my location. The individuals in question consistently evoked a resemblance to scorpions, a comparison that seemed appropriate given my perception of them as being inferior to insects. Upon Lorsan's arrival in close proximity to my location, I proceeded to do a final visual examination of the surrounding atmosphere. As a result of this assessment, I reached a state of contentment with regards to our successful defense against the most recent perilous encounter. Lorsan and I subsequently transitioned back into our humanoid state.

I expressed that their actions are becoming more audacious. Typically, they do not frequently extend their presence to such distances.

Lorsan expressed agreement by nodding. Indeed, this statement holds true. The individuals in question likely have the belief that they are in proximity to achieving the liberation of the aforementioned individual.

It is imperative to express a collective desire for the falsity of the aforementioned statement, as its veracity would result in significant adverse consequences for all those involved.

We positioned ourselves in close proximity within the obscurity of the nocturnal environment, gazing downwards at the lifeless form of our vanquished adversary. Gradually, he transitioned from his draconic manifestation, unveiling a youthful male figure characterized by dark hair, fair complexion, and striking emerald eyes.

I whispered, expressing my observation of his youthful age.

You were of a relatively young age when war was thrust upon you. This phenomenon is a pervasive aspect of our global society, causing me to express concern. At least from our perspective.

Lorsan's age exceeded mine by a span of several centuries. The individual exhibited a high level of resilience and physical prowess as a result of his extensive combat experience. The individual exhibited a profound level of cynicism, yet possessed a notable degree of wisdom. He exhibited a greater degree of loneliness than any other I had encountered, choosing to seclude himself in isolation. He had served as both a companion and a guide in my life, and despite lacking a familial connection, he had become akin to a brother figure over an extensive duration. Lorsan was the individual on this planet whom I held the highest regard for in terms of both affection and trust.

We embodied the characteristics of warriors. The dragons belonging to the N'garth clan. Despite lacking awareness of our presence, we undertook the responsibility of safeguarding humanity against malevolent entities such as the D'naro. We served as an imperceptible barrier safeguarding the realm of humanity from the havoc, devastation, and fatality that would be unleashed upon the planet by the malevolent factions, were they to remain uncontrolled.

I glanced towards Lorsan and experienced a widening of my ocular organs. You appear to be injured.

The individual observed the laceration on his side, as well as the blood that was gradually emerging from his wound, and nonchalantly disregarded it. A sense of fear permeated my being, as I comprehended the implications of the situation.

It is of no significance. I have experienced more unfavorable circumstances in the past. The statement "It's fine" is deemed acceptable.

Lorsan, are you experiencing anger? The injury sustained can be attributed to the sting of a D'naro organism.

The individual's facial expression conveyed a lack of understanding or comprehension in response to my verbal communication. I expressed my disagreement by shaking my head and proceeded to firmly grasp his upper arm, applying a gentle shaking motion.

I cautioned my brother about the lethality of the venom contained within those stingers. Currently, the toxic substance is actively progressing through your physiological system. Failure to administer appropriate medical treatment may result in mortality.

Lorsan casually glanced at the injury, displaying a careless attitude. Upon his gaze returning to me, I discerned a weariness and acceptance reflected in his eyes that instilled inside me a profound sense of fear.

The individual expressed, "I have resided for a considerable duration, Dain." Throughout my recollection, I have consistently been engaged in a state of conflict.

The ongoing struggle persists, my sibling. Your presence is urgently required in a conflict. Is it plausible to assume that our allies will maintain their loyalty in the event that you are not leading our clan?

He placed his hand onto my shoulder and gazed intently into my eyes. You possess exceptional leadership qualities. An exceptional combatant. You are held in high regard by the various clans.

I expressed my disagreement by shaking my head. I do not possess the same level of respect as you do. I will never engage in such behavior. You possess an esteemed reputation, yet I am but a lesser figure in comparison, akin to a sibling of the aforementioned legend.

Subsequently, it may be opportune for you to emerge from obscurity and establish a personal narrative of great significance.

I vigorously shook my head once more, displaying a heightened level of intensity. The current circumstances are not conducive for pursuing such course of action. There is a significant amount of potential consequences involved. In the event that the D'naro faction, together with their supporters, successfully liberate the wizard and release their multitude of demonic progeny, the preservation of our globe would be rendered unfeasible, hence necessitating our defense efforts to become futile.

A little smile appeared on Lorsan's lips. The opportune moment will perpetually elude us, younger sibling. It is imperative to promptly seize the opportunity when it presents itself.

The third point of consideration is as follows. Returning to the Omega

Jeremy was awakened by the streaming sunshine that entered through the windows. The individual displayed a facial expression characterized by the upward curvature of the lips, accompanied by the act of extending the body while situated beneath multiple layers of insulating fabric. Jeremy, being the omega of his werewolf pack, enjoyed numerous privileges, one of which was his exemption from the necessity of employment. The act of rising from bed prior to sunrise was not obligatory, unless one desired to do so or was fulfilling their role and bringing satisfaction to the alpha and/or beta werewolf.

The responsibility of doing such task was assigned to the individual known as the omega. The individual's primary objectives encompass stress reduction, attainment of sexual gratification, and the overall satisfaction of the pack's two most influential leaders. He found solace in this place, where individuals sought refuge from the burdens of society, and he derived immense pleasure from each passing moment.

Today held a significant significance. In the morning, it was customary for Leyton, the beta of the pack, to often visit Jeremy. The individual said that engaging in sexual activity in the morning held a comparable, if not superior, level of significance compared to consuming a morning cup of coffee. Jeremy harbored a profound affection for the large, sociable individual and aspired to fulfill his every desire to the furthest extent. Leyton had been absent for approximately one week due to his involvement in pack-related matters, and today marked his initial day of return to his place of residence.

During their interactions, Leyton would allocate exclusive time to engage with Jeremy, the pack alpha. Notably, Stryker, a male individual recognized by their pack's appellation, approached

Jeremy solely in the company of Leyton. During each occurrence of the full moon, Stryker and Leyton consistently accompanied Jeremy, with additional instances of their companionship on several other nights. Leyton would frequently approach Jeremy alone throughout the morning hours and occasionally throughout the day.

Jeremy ambulated through the residence. The sole article of clothing adorning his person was his omega collar. The object in question consisted of multiple segments of leather that were intricately fastened together in a knot formation. Attached to this arrangement was a brass pendant, prominently showcasing the logo associated with the pack. During all occasions save for his monthly video chat with his parents and siblings, he was devoid of clothing. In addition to this, he would only wear clothing when departing from his residence in the presence of either Stryker or Leyton.

The remainder of his time was dedicated to solitary activities at this location. The architectural layout of his residence included an open form, characterized by expansive windows that facilitated ample natural illumination. Additionally, the house was encompassed by a continuous veranda, encircling three of its sides. The premises featured well-maintained gardens and meticulously manicured lawns, all encompassed by a dense forested area. The entirety of Jeremy's property was fully encompassed by an electrified enclosure. The security system was of exceptional quality both internally and outside. He lacked nothing and was constantly shielded. The presence of cameras throughout the residence enabled Stryker and Leyton to monitor his activities at their convenience. Leyton and Jeremy may have engaged in solitary interactions, yet the absence of privacy is evident due to Stryker's frequent observation of their endeavors. He could be perceived as a prisoner by certain individuals. Jeremy possessed superior knowledge. He was seen as a valuable asset, comparable to a masterpiece that required continuous protection. The installation of a fence and implementation of various security measures were undertaken with the primary objective of ensuring the safety and well-being of Jeremy throughout the entirety of his presence.

Jeremy dedicated a portion of his time to completing his meal orders for the upcoming week. The individual in question possessed a retinue of attendants who catered to his every requirement. The staff of chefs responsible for the preparation of his food were highly valued and esteemed. Prior to assuming the role of the omega, Jeremy's dietary intake primarily of hot dogs, boxed noodles, and fried chicken strips. The individuals responsible for maintaining the cleanliness of his residence and ensuring the delivery of his food and essential items were werewolves who held the highest level of confidence from Stryker packs. Additionally, they were the sole individuals granted access to the facility.

The weather today was pleasant; nonetheless, Jeremy expressed skepticism about his likelihood of spending a significant amount of time outdoors, aside from having breakfast on the porch. It is improbable that Leyton had experienced significant sexual gratification throughout his vacation, except from self-stimulation. The beta member of the pack would exhibit a negative emotional state and require much care and attention. He received more than his usual morning sexual encounter.

Jeremy was already mentally aroused by the anticipation of Leyton's imminent arrival. The individual directed their gaze towards their lap, although observation was the sole action they were capable of undertaking. Jeremy was prohibited from engaging in any form of self-touch except for the purpose of preparing himself. Under the supervision of Stryker and Leyton, the individual ensured that his body remained devoid of hair, even his genitalia, which lacked the natural covering of fur due to regular waxing procedures.

After consuming his morning meal, consisting of coffee and breakfast, the individual concluded the dining experience by placing the dishes on the porch table, with the intention of having them attended to at a later time by a member of the staff. Jeremy returned to the bedroom section. Stryker had expressed amusement and issued a caution to Jeremy over Leyton's inclination towards embracing artificial aids and relying on external objects, in contrast to Stryker's preference for a more organic approach that emphasizes physical prowess. The site contained a bondage crucifix dedicated to Saint Andrew, accompanied by a wooden horse, as well as a set of pulleys and slings situated along one side. Leyton frequently utilized these apparatuses, demonstrating both frequent usage and a notable level of ingenuity.

The individuals engage in a mutual gaze from opposite ends of the room, exhibiting a lack of physical motion. The sun is positioned at a low angle in the window, indicating a limited duration for their forthcoming interaction. There exists a conflict that needs to be addressed, a group that requires reconciliation, and an argument that demands attention. However, prior to delving into the main topic, it is essential to address a preliminary matter.

In a synchronized manner, they remove their garments, carefully placing them in an orderly fashion upon the backrest of a chair. Two male genitalia in an erect state, accompanied by two chests exhibiting rapid and intense movements indicative of heightened physiological arousal, belonging to two individuals whose physical forms are on the verge of intertwining. Jesse's gaze encompasses him, referring to the boy who has deeply impacted his emotions and cognitive processes. The subject possesses an aesthetically pleasing appearance, resembling a sculpture crafted from granite, exuding sensuality and an insatiable desire.

Kit initiates the interaction by placing his hands in Jesse's hair and engaging in a passionate kiss. Jesse embraces his exposed back, drawing him closer, resulting in their respective anatomical structures making contact with their legs, causing friction between them. Jesse emits a vocal expression of pleasure, his physical state already consumed by intense emotion. He exhibits a lively and dynamic demeanor, characterized by an abundance of energy and a sense of eager anticipation.

Kit forcefully positions Jesse on the bed, placing him on his back, and assumes a squatting position, aligning his genitalia with Jesse's posterior along the bed. He expels saliva onto his palm and proceeds to apply it along his firm and noteworthy appendage. As Kit enters the scene, they engage in manual stimulation of Jesse's genitalia. Jesse supports himself with his elbows as he observes the remarkable boy engaging in sexual intercourse with him on two occasions, admiring the skillful manner in which his hands navigate around his physique. He experiences a sudden eruption of goosebumps, causing him to struggle to maintain his concentration.

Kit exhibits a forceful demeanor towards him, forcefully striking his thighs and engaging in intimate activities with a level of intensity that even Jesse finds surprising. Jesse forcefully displaces Kit, resulting in Kit being propelled towards the wall. He initiates physical contact by swiftly moving towards him, firmly placing his lips onto Kit's, and engaging in a biting action. The objects roll haphazardly off the dresser surface and ultimately come to rest on the floor, engaging in a struggle for dominance. Kit emerges victorious once more, compelling Jesse to assume a quadrupedal position. He once again seizes him, injecting surges of warmth into Jesse's bloodstream. He emits vocalizations and exhibits physical resistance in response to the penetration of a male reproductive organ, engaging in vigorous pelvic movements. Kit forcefully disengages and strikes him on the posterior before promptly reinserting himself.

Jesse becomes fatigued from enduring the panting and snarling for several additional minutes. The individual rotates swiftly and brings Kit down to a kneeling position. He forcefully seizes his opponent by the neck and proceeds to bite his lower lip, subsequently positioning Kit in a quadrupedal stance. The individual in question refrains from applying lubrication to their penis, opting instead to insert it forcefully, resulting in a potentially life-threatening experience due to the overwhelming stimulation of the nerve endings within the penis. Kit vocalizes loudly, and his vocalizations evoke the innate animalistic nature within him, yearning to be unleashed.

Kit engages in another altercation with Jesse, resulting in a physical struggle on the floor. Eventually, Jesse gains control and assumes a dominant position with Kit positioned on his lap, engaging in a sexual act. The individuals engage in forceful physical actions, including thrusting, biting, and fighting, until Kit reaches a climax on Jesse's chest. However, Jesse's involvement is not yet concluded. The individual seizes Kit's hair and forcefully tilts their head backwards, subsequently sinking their teeth into Kit's neck. Subsequently, he forcefully brings him down to the ground and assumes a dominant position, engaging in a repetitive motion with his genitalia between his hands until he reaches climax, resulting in the release of semen onto Kit's facial area.

He falls to the ground beside Kit, breathing heavily. Kit ingests a droplet of seminal fluid from his lips and emits a raspy chuckle. The experience was highly demanding.

The experience was highly impressive. Jesse proceeds to roll up his pants and skillfully slides his legs into them. That was an exemplary performance.

You appear to have a preference for engaging in more intense or physically demanding activities.

You derive pleasure from engaging in more intense or forceful interactions.

Kit assumes an upright position and proceeds to cleanse his face using Jesse's shirt. There are no grievances expressed in this statement.

The individuals attire themselves quietly, and Jesse proceeds to release the latch securing his door. Are you prepared for this evening?

Are you?

Jesse emits a chuckle. I am prepared for any situation. Gene is incapable of defeating me.

Let us remain optimistic that your assertion is accurate.

Do you believe that I am incapable of defeating him? Jesse gazes intently at Kit, experiencing a sense of uncertainty regarding whether to interpret Kit's behavior as potentially distressing or as an expression of genuine empathy and concern.

It is acknowledged that you possess the ability to accomplish the task at hand. I am concerned about the well-being and safety of Gene. Kit comes to a halt. Will you refrain from causing harm to him?

Jesse emits a sigh. The response provided by the user is a concise negation.

Jesse proceeds to join the rest of the individuals in the living room, steadfastly disregarding the perceptive expressions directed towards them by Meg and Marque.

May I inquire about the current whereabouts of Gene?

The individual is situated within the confines of his personal living space.

The individual has the capability to rendezvous with us at that location. Jesse proceeds to perform a cervical spine manipulation and engages in a series of stretching exercises. He is enthusiastic and prepared for this event to take place. Harriet's assertion that a satisfactory sexual encounter was the sole requirement for his well-being was accurate. The individual's sensory faculties are finely tuned and prepared for any situation. Gene should express his reliance on Meg's ability to provide medical assistance following this situation. Meg and Marque are capable of extracting him. Harriet and Kit, please proceed.

Eli endeavored to construct an article based on his limited knowledge of the town. The individual perused the concise article, expressing disapproval at its irrationality, and proceeded to eliminate all of its contents.

Regrettably, the individual possessing the most comprehensive knowledge of the town had deliberately evaded any interaction with him throughout the entire day. Nathan departed earlier in the morning without uttering a single word. The individual with whom he was staying exhibited a tendency towards brevity in his speech, prompting him to contemplate the possibility of extracting the desired information from him.

Eli was aware that his culinary abilities were subpar. The individual prepared a chicken stir fry that, unexpectedly, exhibited a pleasing taste. While perusing his emails, he consumed his meal. He made the decision to remain awake until Nathan arrived. It is possible that he would receive compensation for his article.

Eli was seated in a hunched position in front of his computer when Nathan entered the room. He lightly tapped his shoulder in order to rouse him from sleep. In the absence of a response, the individual uttered the subject's name in a gentle manner.

Nathan had not previously encountered an individual who exhibited a profound state of sleep and displayed an endearing appearance during this period. The individual contemplated the act of transporting the person in question to their sleeping quarters, yet recognized that such an action would likely give rise to numerous inquiries upon the arrival of the following day.

He once again vocalized the name "Eli."

Eli awoke with a sense of reluctance. The individual engaged in the act of rubbing their eyes in order to acclimate themselves to their immediate environment. Nathan positioned himself in close proximity, exhibiting a perplexed expression with a smile. Eli promptly raised his hand to his face. The individual expressed a desire to ascertain the absence of desiccated saliva on the aforementioned object.

Does the bed fail to provide sufficient comfort? Nathan engaged in teasing behavior.

Eli responded with a dismissive gesture, accompanied by a sarcastic chuckle. I had been anticipating your arrival.

What is the rationale behind this? The individual proceeded to lightly rub the posterior region of his neck.

I desired to conduct an interview with you. Individuals refrained from speaking to me. Temporarily, Eli briefly perceived a subtle manifestation of dissatisfaction flickering in Nathan's gaze, although it swiftly dissipated, vanishing as swiftly as it had materialized.

The individual responded with a sheepish smile. The individual lacked confidence in their ability to withhold information from Eli, as it aligned with their primal instincts. He had a strong desire to be acknowledged and cherished.

"I will facilitate introductions to individuals who possess comprehensive knowledge," he stated, contemplating the inclusion of his sister.

Eli's countenance displayed a combination of gratitude and enthusiasm, indicating a positive reception to the proposition.

Nathan made a suggestion that the individual should consider going to sleep, as it is likely that they are experiencing fatigue.

My auditory senses are the only ones experiencing fatigue. The individual chuckled as they remarked that Mrs. Hyde exhibited a persistent inclination to engage in conversation concerning topics of a highly unconventional nature.

"I must inform you that you should have listened to her," he concluded.

Nathan effectively suppressed his vocal expression. Mrs. Hyde harbored suspicions regarding the existence of supernatural phenomena, yet her concerns were largely disregarded by others. The individual in question had engaged in multiple instances of impassioned speech, wherein they accused him of belonging to the realm of mythical creatures. However, he responded to these allegations with amusement and did not take them seriously.

The perception of others was that she exhibited signs of mental instability. It would be necessary for him to maintain vigilant observation of her. He shifted his gaze and noticed that Eli was observing him with great focus.

"Could you please repeat that?" he inquired, tilting his head to one side.

Eli inquired about the individual's well-being, noting a slight pallor in their complexion as he gestured towards their face.

The person had a speech impediment while expressing a desire for hydration.

The individual rose from their seat with the intention of retrieving a glass, but, Eli preemptively acquired it before they could do so.

Eli offered the water to him, leading to a momentary contact between their fingers when exchanging it. Once again, the individual experienced a reemergence of the perception of low temperature that had been encountered during their original interaction. The individual's digits remained in contact momentarily, relishing the sensation of Eli's frigid hand against their own.

A profound exchange of glances ensued between them, characterized by an unwavering commitment to maintain eye contact. The individuals experienced a sensation akin to encountering one another for the initial occasion, as if some imperceptible influence compelled their mutual attraction. Nathan momentarily shifted his focus to his lips before returning his look to his eyes.

The individual gently placed their hand on Eli's face, using their thumb to caress his cheekbone. Eli held his breath in anticipation. Nathan's lips were in close proximity, approximately one inch apart. The individual shut their eyes and inclined towards the pink lips that were eagerly anticipating their contact. Upon the gentlest contact of their lips, Eli abruptly recoiled, perceiving a fleeting yet intense surge of sensation, causing Eli to question its reality.

Nathan enveloped Eli in an embrace by encircling his arm around Eli's waist, so reducing the distance between them. Subsequently, Nathan inclined his head and initiated physical contact by pressing his lips against Eli's. Eli derived immense pleasure from the soft and unhurried nature of his partner's kiss, relishing in the display of affectionate care. Nathan gradually intensified the kiss, resulting in an audible expression of pleasure from his partner. Eli succumbed to a pliant state as he was embraced, experiencing a deliberate and measured kiss.

Eli emerged from the kiss in a state of bewilderment, still contemplating the stark contrast of the experience. The individual's heightened sense of joy quickly diminished upon observing the countenance of Nathan. The emotional response seen encompassed a combination of alarm, perplexity, and regret. He experienced the sensation of his arm, which had before been engaged in an ardent embrace, descending.

Tanner rotated his cranium and emitted a yawn. If only we had a greater amount of time to remain in a recumbent position in our beds. Is it not expected that sheriffs in small towns allocate a greater portion of their time to leisurely pursuits? I have not had the opportunity to engage in leisurely activities for several months.

"We are currently residing in a period of great significance," Van responded, going closer to engage in a prolonged kiss with his partner. Therefore, should we prolong our stay in Arizona for a few more days, or should we proceed to Grand Junction with the intention of intercepting the perpetrators en route, all the while ensuring the rescue of Parker?

Tanner emitted a sigh while compressing his lips. Parker should redirect his focus towards returning to the Hardwood and refrain from engaging in rescue operations, as those responsibilities are more suited for our team.

Van expressed his disagreement by shaking his head. I am aware of the situation, however, I am also cognizant of Parker's strong desire to provide assistance to us and the broader shifter community. The concern is in my desire to prevent any harm from befalling him.

I also desire to prevent any harm from befalling him. Tanner gently passed his hands through Van's hair. Therefore, I prefer that he remains in Hardwood. Even in that particular context, he possesses the ability to contribute significantly in a beneficial manner.

The individual possesses awareness of the aforementioned fact, nevertheless harbors a desire to engage in more actions or endeavors. Van was uncertain about how to present a persuasive argument in support of Parker's viewpoint on the matter of providing assistance. Following the incident in Las Vegas, the individuals in question had a noticeable tendency to engage in frequent discussions over the event, particularly during their private interactions. Parker exhibited a reluctance to consistently broach the subject with the wolf, Tanner, in order to avoid causing distress or agitation. Many residents of Hardwood opted to relocate to Van rather than Tanner due to their unfamiliarity with handling predatory animals.

Let us observe the unfolding events of the day. Tanner engaged in a physical act of affection by kissing Van. If our hypothesis is accurate, the mountain lion and the majority of their population have migrated in the direction of Grand

Junction. It would be advisable for us to proceed in that direction as well.

Would you like me to initiate a phone call to Parker? Van briefly glanced at the clock. At the present moment, given the early hour, it is probable that the individual's acquaintance is still in a state of repose, unless there are any significant events or circumstances that would necessitate their immediate attention.

Tanner embraced Van. Once we have completed our shower, we can proceed to contact him. It is possible that he may possess news at that point as well. Following an exchange of affectionate gestures, he emitted a sigh. It might be advisable to contact Felipe in order to ascertain whether anyone has made contact with him.

Van expressed agreement by nodding. It is important to remember that Steven also has to be included and engaged in the task at hand.

Indeed. Tanner tilted his head inquisitively. I believe I perceive auditory indications of activity emanating from his quarters. It is highly likely that he has already awakened.

The given utterance appears to be indicative of the individual named Steven. Occasionally, there was a discernible disparity in the upbringing of Parker and his sibling, giving the impression that they were offspring of dissimilar progenitors. In addition to their respective supernatural abilities as a shifter and a magician, it appeared that Steven has an exceptional capacity to function without sufficient sleep, whilst Parker exhibited a preference for a bright and warm environment to initiate his daily activities.

Van exerted his willpower to maneuver his body away from Tanner's and proceeded towards the bathroom in order to initiate the showering process. Similar to Tanner, he would have great joy in remaining in bed for an extended period and commencing his day with leisurely activities.

Tanner's mobile device emitted an audible sound, coinciding with Van's act of donning his trousers. The general tone employed by Tanner was unfamiliar to Van, thus indicating that the individual was not recognizable based on their ring.

Tanner promptly swiped the phone to respond. Hello, Felipe.

Van reclined onto the bed and attentively listened, well aware of Tanner's indifference.

I do not possess any novel information to present to you at this time; but, I surmise that you may find it of interest to be informed that, in the event that you were contemplating the prospect of prolonging your stay for a few additional days, this information may be of relevance to you.

We appreciate your notification. Tanner positioned himself adjacent to Van, inadvertently making contact with his leg. In the event of an unforeseen circumstance, it is possible for us to alter our course and return to our original starting point. If the situation is significant, there is a possibility that Steven could facilitate my return to this location, while Van assumes the responsibility of driving back.

Van had not previously considered this matter, and he found it unfavorable. In the event that Tanner were to confront the hunters, he expressed a desire to stand at his side. The collective survival prospects of the individuals were higher when they were in close proximity to one another, as opposed to being separated.

Are there not advantages to having magicians present? Felipe emitted a light-hearted laugh.

I am currently engaged in the process of acquiring knowledge and skills. Tanner had a facial expression characterized by a smile.

A distinct sound of knocking emanated from the entrance.

Van hesitated momentarily before proceeding towards it. The auditory perception of Steven's movements in the neighboring room was not discernible to him. The auditory perception of the heart's pulsation emanating from the entrance exhibited characteristics akin to those typically associated with human auditory stimuli. The individual in question may potentially be Steven, or alternatively, it may be another individual.

In a deliberate manner, Van proceeded across the room. Recognizing that his level of unease exceeded what would often be expected in a conventional motel room. The hunters were inadvertently activating certain mechanisms without conscious awareness. Would Van be able to identify his own identity after the hunters were apprehended? Despite the passage of several months, the individual who was formerly characterized by a carefree and optimistic demeanor has now exhibited a heightened sense of caution. Indeed, every individual belonging to the shifter community was instructed to exercise caution in their interactions with humans and to refrain from disclosing their true nature. However, the situation at hand surpassed these general guidelines. The individual expressed a dislike for experiencing a heightened state of alertness and tension. The instances in which he and Tanner would recline on the couch at his residence, seemingly unconcerned about the potential arrival of armed individuals intent on causing harm, provided a pleasant respite, serving as a personal sanctuary within a reality that had unexpectedly become significantly bleaker than his previous expectations.

Vincent did not fail to acknowledge the gesture of Dante's extensive provision of backup personnel. However, he did express a desire for prior notification from Dante, allowing him to procure a more capacious vehicle. Incorporating that particular group proved to be challenging.

The individual had been contemplating the challenges associated with commanding a pack of wolves belonging to a different Alpha during combat. Shortly thereafter, an opportunity to assess his leadership skills presented itself. The car contained a total of five seats, with two located in the front and three in the rear. The individual, along with five other wolves, occupied the car.

Vincent initially contemplated allowing the parties involved to resolve the matter independently; but, their incessant bickering proved to be excessively time-consuming, prompting him to reconsider his stance.

As his emotional state intensified, he had a sensation of mental stimulation. The physical contact had persisted since the moment when he and Karl had openly expressed their emotions to one another. The experience provided a sense of comfort and tranquility, whilst fostering resilience.

Rhiannon is positioned at the front. The remaining individuals should strive to improve their physical fitness. Please proceed with the task at hand.

The individual's vocal expression exhibited a resolute and unwavering demeanor, demonstrating a conviction in the correctness of their decision. Rhiannon held the position of being Dante's second, so warranting a higher level of respect compared to the remaining individuals. The limited space in the rear seating area would pose a challenge, yet the individuals involved would find a way to accommodate themselves and persevere.

Initially, the individuals directed their gaze towards him, exhibiting a lack of enthusiasm in response to being subjected to the commands of an additional dominant individual. Vincent maintained a commanding demeanor via his facial expressions and body language, while also recognizing that Dante likely instructed his subordinates to adhere to his directives.

In due course, and very expeditiously, they accomplished the task.

One individual transformed into the shape of a wolf, while the remaining three individuals gathered their belongings. The wolf assumed a seated position on their laps, and in the event that their return to town was observed, it would merely appear as though they were accompanied by their canine companion. The dog in question is of considerable size and magnitude. If they refrain from scrutinizing the subject matter, it would appear entirely ordinary.

One obstacle has been overcome. Vincent estimated that the remaining number of tasks to be completed by the conclusion of the night was approximately 500,000.

The user's text does not contain any information to be rewritten.

As per his usual routine, Vincent parked his vehicle a few streets away. The Hamilton base possessed a quite distinctive characteristic in that it was situated within the confines of New York City itself, thereby offering a notable degree of convenience at the time. Within the confines of the parking garage, the lupine being underwent a metamorphic process, enabling it to don its attire and then engage in the unassuming act of assimilating with the pedestrian populace traversing the adjacent streets. Even during the late hours of the night or early hours of the morning, there were individuals present in the vicinity.

Vincent assumed the role of the leader, exhibiting heightened sensory awareness. The protagonist detected the presence of human adrenaline at the base, in significant quantities. This prompted him to contemplate the nature of the situation and the potential consequences of his leadership of the unfamiliar wolves.

Silently, he approached the concealed location where the fence had been breached. Prior to his arrival, he detected the scent of David and Pat, but not Cory. This may not be advantageous.

Upon nearing the scene, the observer noticed the presence of two individuals exhibiting signs of heightened anticipation. He prioritized taking the lead in order to communicate to the others that the presence of these unfamiliar wolves did not constitute an encroachment into their established domain. Despite this, the observer remained confident in his perception of perceiving a distinct sense of defiance reflected in the gazes of the other members of his wolf pack.

Whom do they refer to? David emitted a low, sibilant sound, displaying his refusal to retreat from the aperture, so compelling the other wolves to enter the opening individually, in a constricted manner. The territorial nature of wolves is noteworthy, making it particularly amazing that Dante allowed the borrowing of members from his pack.

Rhiannon expressed her opinion of David's demeanor as being highly courteous, yet with a hint of contempt. Vincent emitted a quiet laughter, notwithstanding the prevailing tension. Alphas were historically recognized for their inclination towards dominance and control. However, it is important to note that Betas also exhibited tendencies of aggression and hostility within their own social dynamics.

Vincent expeditiously elucidated that Rhiannon is present to provide assistance, courtesy of her Alpha. Similarly, the remaining wolves also exhibit this characteristic. It is imperative that we expedite our actions. The current whereabouts of Cory and the current status of the girl's whereabouts remain unknown.

Pat observed the intense confrontation between Rhiannon and David with a sense of pleasure, although this expression quickly vanished from his countenance upon being asked a direct question.

Cory has departed. It is believed that Whitaker has apprehended him.

The prognosis for her condition is positive. The speaker expressed his frustration to the audience, acknowledging the occurrence of several fractures.

Mara and Zena hastily approached Tabitha, exhibiting gentle pawing and sniffing behaviors similar to those previously demonstrated by Daniel. Mara expressed her disappointment by shaking her head in a rueful manner.

"That was completely inappropriate," she muttered to Daniel. The wolf belonging to the protagonist conveyed a narrative that was substantially identical to the one depicted in Dirk's hasty video montage.

Daniel exclaimed loudly, urging everyone's attention, and reassured that Tabitha's well-being is guaranteed. I will transport her to my residence and proceed with the process of realigning the fractured bones. She will be prepared to proceed within a few days.

Both Zena and Dirk expressed their agreement by nodding, despite their reluctance to part with her. However, they recognized that Daniel was the most suitable one to provide care for her. Crane had dedicated his entire healing expertise to Daniel, although he had not been required to employ it until the present moment. The lingering impact of Crane's trust and regard continued to resonate inside the collective awareness of the group. Furthermore, due to her werewolf regenerative capabilities, she would only need to endure a limited period of discomfort.

Loud footfalls resonated across the veranda as the entrance forcefully swung ajar. Francine assumed a defensive stance at the entrance, extending her arms outward, while audibly exhaling and emitting aggressive vocalizations in her anthropomorphic state. She proceeded to transition between her lupine and human forms intermittently. Daniel approached the space separating Francine and Tabitha with purposeful strides, assuming a half-crouched position, prepared to engage in combat with her in either of her possible forms.

Francine transitioned into a human form, her teeth audibly clenching. She issued a demand for him to move aside, while attempting to maneuver around him. Daniel effortlessly interrupted her once more.

Mara, please retrieve Francine's vest and promptly escort her away from this location.

Daniel averted his eyes, partially adjusting his position while allowing his wolf to emit a menacing snarl and growl. Francine assumed an upright posture and narrowed her eyes, engaging in a process of mental computation.

Francine expressed her discontent by remarking, "She appropriated my target," while swiftly donning her leather vest.

Daniel expressed his disagreement by shaking his head. The significance of the topic is inconsequential. Please return to your place of residence.

The topic at hand is of significance. I will not tolerate disrespect from a somebody of lesser stature."

Francine displayed a threatening facial expression by exposing her teeth and emitting a low, guttural sound, while simultaneously exhibiting signs of heavy breathing and a flushed complexion. Daniel hesitated, attempting to evaluate the circumstances while preventing her from launching another assault on Tabitha.

The group gradually moved closer, demonstrating support for Daniel without engaging in direct confrontation.

I am the mate of the Alpha. Francine expressed her bitterness as she reminded everyone. Daniel chose to ignore the insult and suppressed his inclination to rectify her statement. If I desire to achieve a successful outcome, I am determined to attain it. It is imperative for all individuals to bear in mind that... The individual gestured at several areas within the space. The individual's hair, which possessed a dark blonde hue, exhibited a disheveled appearance, with strands protruding in various directions. Additionally, droplets of perspiration descended along her forehead. The wolf belonging to Daniel provided counsel regarding the importance of exercising prudence.

Francine," he uttered in a subdued and gentle tone, "You may address that matter with Grant. He will attentively consider your perspective. Currently, my primary objective is to ensure the safe return of Tabitha and provide her with appropriate care. It is advisable that you depart.

Francine exhibited signs of restlessness as she paced back and forth, displaying physical manifestations of anxiety through the repetitive clenching and unclenching of her fists.

Zena and I were in the process of departing, Francine. Why do you not accompany us? Dirk provided assistance in a helpful manner.

I refuse to engage in conversation conducted in such a disrespectful manner. Francine expressed intense anger without directing it towards any specific individual. Please exercise caution, Daniel. I am aware of your tendency to consistently involve yourself in various situations, actively inserting yourself into the midst of affairs, and successfully attaining desired outcomes. Please exercise caution and be mindful of your actions. If one believes oneself to be deserving of the position I hold within this group, it can be considered an irrational belief.

The expression of affection towards another individual is conveyed by the phrase "I love you."

Upon hearing Michael softly utter those aesthetically pleasing three words, I found myself expressing gratitude to the divine being responsible for creating an individual of such impeccable physical appearance and allure. The individual has a short hairstyle, with dark brown hair that seemed black in low light conditions, thus enhancing the definition of his jawline. The individual's deep blue eyes, which might be misconstrued as black by an uninformed observer, were directed at me.

I reciprocate the sentiment, Michael. I ultimately verbalized my sentiments and engaged in a kiss with his resplendent crimson lips. I have eagerly anticipated that time for an extended duration, and it was widely recognized throughout the cosmos the extent to which I was deeply enamored with him. Emotions such as fear, resentment, and rejection constituted significant barriers that rendered the act of expressing my affection towards Michael unattainable. The experience of being homosexual is often fraught with challenges, as individuals frequently have difficulties in attaining acceptance from both their social circle and immediate relatives. The role of society is of great importance, and it was evident to me that a tiny town in Ohio would not be receptive to an individual such as myself. The presence of fear hindered my ability to express to Michael the depth of my affection for him, which had been ignited at our initial encounter.

However, any feelings of bitterness and sorrow were dissipated as I experienced a sweet sensation on my taste buds. The individual possessed a dark complexion, impeccably styled hair, attractive lips, and striking blue eyes, in addition to a well-defined physique and sculpted chest. These physical attributes encompassed all the qualities I desired. I found it incredulous that, despite the passage of a significant duration, he had become my possession. I am solely extracting resources.

Rise and shine, you individual of questionable intelligence! Upon awakening, I perceived the auditory presence of my English instructor.

I was aware that it was a dream. The possibility of Michael and I being together seemed unattainable, leading me to believe that it must have been a mere dream. It is highly unlikely to occur throughout the duration of an individual's lifespan.

Whom was I deceiving? What were the factors that contributed to my susceptibility to deception?

I expressed self-reproach on multiple occasions upon regaining complete cognitive awareness and endeavored to formulate a justification.

I apologize, sir. I expressed my physical discomfort," I stated, directing my gaze towards Michael, who was situated in close proximity, exhibiting a lack of awareness regarding my internal state.

Tony, please be advised that this serves as your final warning. Mr. Sanders, my instructor, expressed his disapproval of the relaxed demeanor exhibited in my classroom, while making an effort to refrain from reprimanding me. It is unlikely that he would exhibit excessive severity, as I am aware. Throughout my academic journey, I have consistently demonstrated exceptional aptitude for learning, which has earned me the distinction of being one of his preferred pupils.

I discreetly observed Michael from my peripheral vision, making a concerted effort to maintain focus on the speech. During our study of A Midsummer Night's Dream, a renowned work by William Shakespeare, I had an unprecedented challenge in maintaining my focus.

What was the subject matter of your dream? Michael, with his distinct Colombian accent, inquired of me.

No. The individual expressed a lack of content or substance in their statement. I made a false statement. I was required to do so.

He commented that the individual's lips were exhibiting a pouting expression similar to that of a cheerleader.

No, I was not. I responded by suggesting that you focus your attention on your book.

I patiently awaited the conclusion of the class session in order to discreetly abscond from the situation that had caused me much humiliation. The events of the day were not favorable to me.

I apologize, but I cannot provide any assistance without any text or information to work with.

Upon the conclusion of the school day, I harbored a strong desire to expeditiously return to my place of residence. I did not feel inclined to socialize with anyone. My primary objective was to return to my place of residence, finalize any outstanding written assignments, and partake in viewing the most recent installment of the television series "Game of Thrones."

My intended course of action for the remainder of the day was as follows. I received a telephone call from an individual named Michael, however, I unwillingly terminated the connection. I was unable to engage in conversation with him subsequent to experiencing such a vivid daydream.

I accessed the Grindr application on my mobile device and proceeded to peruse many user profiles. The display appeared inactive, with identical images and profiles. At the age of eighteen, I experienced a profound sense of despair, as if my existence had reached its ultimate conclusion. During my last year of secondary education, when my peers were occupied with completing their college applications, I found myself engaged in the process of determining my future aspirations.

Throughout my personal history, I have only engaged in romantic relationships with individuals of the same gender, since I have been cognizant of my sexual orientation as a homosexual individual for as long as I can recall. In my personal history, I have had an attraction towards numerous individuals of the male gender. However, it is noteworthy to mention that none of these encounters have resulted in a lasting and indelible impact on my memory or emotions. I have engaged in intimate encounters with individuals whom I did not have prior acquaintance with, as well as pursued romantic relationships with individuals without any expectations of commitment. However, these endeavors did not yield satisfactory outcomes. I possessed a countenance that lacked distinctiveness, characterized by fair-colored hair, and an appearance that could be considered ordinary. I endeavored to enhance my physique and cultivate a more athletic aesthetic, and I am gratified to observe discernible alterations in my physical appearance. The desire for perpetual longevity motivated me, and I recognized the unlikelihood of discovering my desired outcome inside the confines of the limited municipality.

Disclosing my sexual orientation to my parents proved to be an exceptionally challenging endeavor, ranking as the most arduous undertaking I have encountered thus far in my existence. I vividly recall the occasion when I disclosed my sexual orientation as a homosexual individual to my father. The sensation of a lump in my throat persists. I am deeply grateful to my parents for expressing unconditional love towards me, since they have consistently assured me of their affection regardless of any circumstances. However, they also conveyed to me that my life would not be characterized by simplicity.

In the town, a significant number of individuals may lack comprehension of your situation or harbor the belief that they possess the ability to rectify it. It is advisable to refrain from engaging with or encountering them. There is a possibility that individuals may experience instances of bullying or encounter a cessation of communication from their peers. However, it is important for you to be aware that we hold a deep and profound affection for you. "We shall perpetually remain available to provide support for you," I recollect my mother articulating as she embraced me with great intensity. The individual expressed sincere intent with each remark, and I was exceptionally blessed to have her presence in my life. It took me a mere few weeks to come to the realization that she was indeed correct. All the information conveyed to me by her occurred in a precise chronological order. I experienced a shift in interpersonal dynamics as individuals who were once considered friends became adversaries, while previously unfamiliar individuals began engaging in acts of harassment without discernible cause. However, during the turmoil's resolution, there remained a solitary companion who remained unchanged - Michael.